Charlie Chaplin's own Story

Charlie Chaplin as camera man

CHARLIE CHAPLIN'S OWN STORY

BEING THE FAITHFUL RECITAL OF A ROMANTIC CAREER,
BEGINNING WITH EARLY RECOLLECTIONS OF BOY-
HOOD IN LONDON AND CLOSING WITH THE
SIGNING OF HIS LATEST MOTION-
PICTURE CONTRACT

ILLUSTRATED WITH PHOTOGRAPHS

INDIANAPOLIS
THE BOBBS-MERRILL COMPANY
PUBLISHERS

The subject of this biography takes great pleasure
in expressing his obligations and his thanks to Mrs.
Rose Wilder Lane for invaluable editorial assistance.

CONTENTS

CONTENTS—Continued

CONTENTS—Continued

CONTENTS—Continued

CHARLIE CHAPLIN'S OWN STORY

CHARLIE CHAPLIN'S OWN STORY

CHAPTER I

In which I relate my experiences up to the age of five; and describe the occasion of my first public appearance on any stage.

LIFE itself is a comedy—a slap-stick comedy at that. It is always hitting you over the head with the unexpected. You reach to get the thing you want—slap! bang! It's gone! You strike at your enemy and hit a friend. You walk confidently, and fall. Whether it is tragedy or comedy depends on how you look at it. There is not a hair's breadth between them.

When I was eleven years old, homeless and starving in London, I had big dreams. I was a precocious youngster, full of imagination and fancies and pride. My dream was to become a great musician, or an actor like Booth. Here I am to-day, becoming a millionaire because I wear funny shoes. Slap-stick comedy, what?

Still, there is not much laughter in the world, and a lot of that is cynical. As long as I can keep people laughing good chuckling laughs I shall be satisfied. I can't keep it up long, of course. The public is like a child; it gets tired of its toys and throws them away. When that happens I shall do something else, and still be satisfied. I always knew that some day I would have my share of the spot-light, and I am having it, so after all I have realized my ambitions.

My mother is proud of it. That is another of life's slap-stick comedies—that my mother, one of the proudest, most gentle women in England, should hope for twenty years that some day I would be a great tragic actor, and now should lie in an English hospital, glad that I am greeted with howls of laughter whenever I appear in comedy make-up on the moving-picture screen.

When I was two or three years old my mother began to be proud of my acting. After she and my father came back from their work in the London music-halls they used to have little parties of friends for supper, and father would come and pull me out of bed to stand on the table and recite for them.

My father was a great, dark, handsome man. He would put me upon his shoulder to bring me out, and I did not like it, because his rough prickly cheek hurt me. Then he would set me upon the table in my nightgown, with the bright lights hurting my eyes, and every one would laugh and tell me to sing for the drops of wine in their glasses. I always did, and the party applauded and laughed and called for more. I could mimic every one I had ever seen and sing all the songs I had heard.

They would keep me doing it for hours, until I got so sleepy I could not stand up and fell over among the dishes. Then. mother picked me up and carried me to bed again. I remember just how her hair fell down over the pillow as she tucked me in. It was brown hair, very soft and perfumed, and her face was so full of fun it seemed to sparkle. That was in the early days, of course.

I do not know my mother's real name. She came of a good respected family in London, and when she was sixteen she ran away and married my father, a music-hall actor. She never heard from her own people again. She drifted over England and the Continent with my father, and went on the music-hall stage herself. They never made much money, and my father spent it all. Most of the time we lived very poorly, in actors' lodgings, and my mother worried about food for us. Then there would be a streak of luck, and we all had new clothes and lived lavishly for a few days.

My brother Sidney was four years old when I was born in a little town in France, between music-hall engagements. As soon as my mother could travel we went back to London, and she went to work again. Her stage name was Lillie Harley, and she was very popular in English music-halls, where she sang character songs. She had a beautiful sweet voice, but she hated the stage and the life. Sometimes at night she came into my bed and cried herself to sleep with her arms around me, and I was so miserable that I wanted to scream, but I did not dare, for fear of waking my father.

He was Charles Chaplin, the singer of descriptive ballads. His voice was a fine bari-

14

tone, and he was a great music-hall success and is still remembered in England. My mother and he were always laughing and singing together, and my mother was very fond of him, but a little afraid, too. When he was angry she grew white and her hands shook. She had thin delicate hands, which reminded me of the claws of some little bird when she dressed me.

In spite of the hit-and-miss life we led, always moving from town to town, and my mother's hard work on the stage and our lack of money, she took pride in keeping my brother and me beautifully dressed. At night, after her music-hall work was done and the party had gone, I woke and saw her pressing out our little white Eton collars and brushing our suits, while every one was asleep.

One day, when I was about five years old, Sidney and I were playing on the floor when my mother came in, staggering. I thought she was drunk. I had seen so many persons drunk it was commonplace to me, but seeing my mother that way was horrible. I opened my mouth and screamed in terror. I screamed and screamed; it seemed as if I could not stop.

Sidney ran out of the room. My mother

15

did not look at me; she stumbled across the room and tried to take off her hat. All her hair came tumbling down over her face, and she fell on the bed.

After a while I crawled over and touched her hand, which hung down. It was cold, and it frightened me so I could not make a sound. I backed under the bed, little by little, until I reached the wall, and sat there, still, staring at my mother's hand.

After a long time the door opened and I saw my father's boots walk in. I heard him swearing. The boots came over and stood by the bed. I smelled whisky, and after a while I heard my mother's voice, very weak.

"Don't be a hysterical fool. You've got to work to-night. We need the money," my father said.

"I can't. I'm not up to it. I'm sick," I heard my mother say, sobbing.

My father's boots stamped up and down the room.

"Well, I'll take Charlie, then," he said. "Where's the brat?"

I backed closer to the wall, and kept still. With no reason, I was terrified. Then the

16

door opened again, my father's boots tramped out and down the stairs, and I heard my mother calling me. I came slowly out from under the bed.

My mother said she wanted me to go on the stage in her place that night and sing my very best. I said I would. Then she had me bring her a little new coat she had made for me, and a fresh collar. She still lay on the bed, and my chin barely came above the edge of it, so it took her a long time to dress me and to get my hair combed to suit her. She was still busy with it when my father came back.

Then she kissed me in a hurry and told me to do my best. My father took my hand and we started to the music-hall. We were at Aldershot, a garrison town, and soldiers were everywhere. I kept tipping my head back to see their uniforms as they passed us, and my father was jerking me along at such a rate my neck nearly snapped in two.

We were late when we reached the music-hall. I had never seen one before; my mother had always put us to bed before she went to work. My father took me down a little alley, through a bare dim place, to one end of the

17

stage. I saw a big crowd on the other side of it—just hundreds of heads massed together. There were music and noise, and the stage was a glare of light.

A girl in tights and shiny spangles came and put grease paint on my cheeks, and when I wanted to rub it off they would not let me. Then it was time for my mother's act, and my father faced me toward the stage and gave me a little push.

"Go out and sing *Jack Jones*," he said.

CHAPTER II

In which I make my first public appearance on the stage and my first success; and meet the red-faced man.

I WALKED uncertainly out on the stage. The glare of the lights dazzled me so I stumbled. The stage seemed a great empty place, and I felt little and alone. I did not know just what to do, but my father had told me to go out and sing *Jack Jones,* and I did not dare go back until I had done it.

There was a great uproar beyond the footlights, and it confused me more, until I saw that the people were laughing and applauding. Then I remembered my singing on the table, with people all around and noise and light, and I saw that this was the same thing. I opened my mouth and sang *Jack Jones* with all my might.

It was an old coster song my father had taught me. I sang one verse and started on the second, hurrying to get through. I was

19

not afraid of the crowd, but the stage got bigger and I got littler every minute, and I wanted to be with my mother.

There was a great noise which interrupted my song, and something hit me on the cheek. I stopped singing with my mouth open on a note, and something else hit the floor by my feet, and then a shower of things fell on the stage and one struck my arm. The audience was throwing them at me.

I backed away a little, terrified, but I went on singing as well as I could, with my face quivering and a big lump in my throat. I knew I had to finish the song because my father had told me to. Great tears came up in my eyes, and I ducked my head and rubbed at them with my knuckles, and then I saw the floor of the stage. It was almost covered with pennies and shillings. Money! It was money they were throwing at me!

"Oh! Wait, wait!" I shouted, and went down on my hands and knees to gather it up. "It's money! Wait just a minute!"

I got both hands full of it, and still there was more. I crawled around, picking it up and putting it in my pockets and shouted at

the audience, "Wait till I get it all and I'll sing a lot!"

It was a great hit. People laughed and ·shouted and climbed on their seats to throw more money. It kept falling around me, rolling across the stage, while I ran after it, shouting with joy. I filled all my pockets and put some in my hat. Then I stood up and sang *Jack Jones* twice, and would have sung it again, but my father came out on the stage and led me off.

I had almost three pounds in six-penny pieces, shillings, and even a few half-crowns. I sat on a box and played with it while my father did his act. I could not count it, but I knew it was money, and I felt rich. Then we went home, where my father set me upon the bed beside my mother, and I poured the money over her, laughing. She laughed, too, and my father took the money and bought us all a great feast, and let me drink some of the ale. I remember how I crowed over Sidney that night.

My mother was able to go back to work next day, and Sidney and I were left in the rooms again. There was a quarrel before she went; my father swore, and mother cried and stamped her foot. She said, "No! No! No! He's too little yet." And I knew they were talking about me, and crawled away into a corner, where I kept very still.

After that I think we grew poorer and poorer. There were no more parties at night. My mother would come in alone, and when she waked me, tucking me in, I felt so sad it seemed as if my heart would break, because her face did not sparkle any more. Sidney and I played about in the daytime, and kept out of father's way. When he came in his face was red, and his breath was hot and strong with whisky. He used to throw himself on the bed without a word to mother and fall asleep with his mouth open. Then Sidney and I went quietly out and played on the stairs. Sidney was a wide-awake lively young person, always running about and shouting "Ship ahoy!" He wanted to be a sailor. I could not play with him long because it tired me. I liked to get into a corner by myself and think and dream of things I had seen and what I would do some day—vague dreams of making music and wearing velvet suits and bowing to immense audiences and having cream tarts for every meal and six white ponies to drive.

The worry and the unhappiness which seemed to grow like a cloud around us in those years made me sit sometimes and cry quietly to myself, not knowing why, but feeling miserable and sad. Then my great dreams faded and I felt little and lonely, and not even my mother could comfort me.

So I came to be about ten years old, and all my memories of the years between my first appearance on the stage and the day I met the red-faced man are vague recollections of these dreams and hurried trips from place to place, and the unhappiness, and my mother's face growing sadder. Then I remember clearly the night I went with her to the music-hall in London and ran away with the clog dancers.

My mother took me with her because when it was time for her to go to work she could not find Sidney. He was almost fourteen and played a great deal in the streets, and used to go away for the whole day sometimes, which worried my mother. But she had to work and could not be with us or keep us together. It is my impression that my father was making

23

very little money then, and spending all he got in bars, as he was a very popular man and had many friends who wanted him to drink with them. I know that we were living in very poor lodgings, and my mother cried sometimes when the landlady asked her for the rent.

I remember on this day standing beside my mother and watching a troupe of clog dancers who were working on the stage. Mother was wearing her stage dress, waiting to go on for her act, and she kept asking me where I had seen Sidney last, but I could hardly listen. I knew how to clog dance, for Sidney and I had done it with the boys in the streets, and I was impatient because my mother had her hand on my shoulder, and I wanted to do the steps with the others. I squirmed away from her and began dancing by myself. I did all the difficult steps very proudly, and when the music stopped I saw that my mother looked proud, too. I looked around to see if any one else was admiring me, and saw the red-faced man.

He was standing behind my mother, a fat man, with a double chin, and a wart on one of his lower eyelids. It fascinated me so I could

24

not take my eyes from it. When my mother went on for her act I still stood staring at it.

"I say, you're lively on your feet, young feller," he said to me. "Could you do that every day, say?"

"Oh, yes, I like to do it," I said.

"Would you like to come along, now, with a nice troupe of fine little boys and do it for a fortnight or so?" he asked.

"What's the screw?" I said, looking shrewd, as I had seen my father do. He laughed.

"Three six a week," he said, "all for your own pocket money. And I'll buy you a velvet suit, and you can eat hearty—meat pies and pudding every meal."

"And cream tarts?" I stipulated.

"Up to your eyes in cream tarts if you like," he said. "Come now, will you do it?"

"Yes," I answered promptly.

"All right, come along," he said, and led me out of the music-hall.

CHAPTER III

In which I join the clog dancers; fail to get the cream
tarts; and incur the wrath of Mr. Hawkins.

WAITING just inside the door to the alley were
the five boys who had been clog dancing. They
were huddled together, not playing or talking,
and when the red-faced man led me up to them
they looked at me curiously, without a word.
Each one had his stage dress in a brown paper
bundle under his arm, and in the gas light they
looked ragged and tired.

"This 'ere's the new little boy what's a-going
to come with us," said the red-faced man, holding my hand so tight it hurt, and I squirmed.

The other boys did not say a word. They
looked at me, and all those staring eyes made
me uncomfortable.

"Speak up, there!" roared the man suddenly,
and they all jumped. "Say 'Yes, sir, yes, Mr.
'Awkins,' when I speak to you!"

"Yes, sir, yes, Mr. 'Awkins!" they all said.

"Now step up, young fellers; we're going to our nice 'ome and 'ave cream tarts for our supper," Mr. Hawkins said. He nodded to the stage doorkeeper, a silent whiskered man who sat smoking a pipe, and we all filed out through the dark little alley into the street.

It was a cold foggy night. The street lamps were weird ghostly-looking blurs in the mist, and our steps sounded hollow and muffled. I had never been out so late before, and the strange look of things in the fog and the emptiness of the streets, with only a cab rattling by now and then, made me shiver.

The boys walked ahead, and Mr. Hawkins and I followed close behind. We walked for a long time, till my legs began to ache and my fingers stopped hurting and grew numb in Mr. Hawkins' hard grip. My mind was all a-muddle and confused, so that the only thing I thought of clearly was my mother, and how pleased she would be when I came home again rich, with three and sixpence and a velvet suit.

We came at last to a doorway with a lamp burning dimly over it, and Mr. Hawkins herded the boys into it. A very fat dirty woman opened the door and said something shrill to us. Then we climbed many flights of dark stairs, and Mr. Hawkins let go my hand to open a door.

A damp musty smell came out as we stumbled in. It was a poor dirty room, furnished with two beds and a long table with chairs about it.

"Well, 'ere we are 'ome!" said Mr. Hawkins cheerfully. "Now for a nice 'ot supper, what?" The boys did not say a word. They sat down and watched him, looking now and then at the door. I rubbed my aching fingers and looked at him, too. The wart was still there on his lower eyelid, and I could not take my eyes from it.

After a while the fat woman came in with our supper—chops and ale for Mr. Hawkins; plates of porridge and thick slices of bread for us. The boys all fell to eating hungrily, but I pushed my plate back and looked at Mr. Hawkins, who was eating his chops and drinking his ale with great enjoyment.

"Where are the cream tarts?" I asked him.

"Cream tarts! Who ever 'eard of cream tarts for supper?" he shouted. "Cream tarts!" He chuckled and repeated it over and over,

28

till I felt ashamed and confused. Then he thrust his great red face almost against mine and roared in a terrible voice, "That's enough, young feller! I'll cream tart you! I'll jolly well cream tart you!" I shrank into my chair, frightened.

"You don't want cream tarts," he said. "You want a caning. You want a good hard caning, don't you?"

"No, sir," I said. "Oh, no, sir, please."

"Oh, you don't, don't you? Yes, you do. You want a caning, that's what you want. Where's my cane?" he roared in a frightful voice. I crouched in my chair in such terrible fear I could not even cry out until his great hand gripped my shoulder. Then I shrieked in agony.

He only shook me and flung me back in the chair, but from that moment I lived in terror of him—a terror that colored everything during the day and at night made my dreams horrible. The other boys were afraid of him, too. When he was with us we sat silent and wary, looking at him. He used to swing his cane as he walked up and down the room in the evenings, and we watched it in fearful fascination, though I do not remember that he ever caned one of us. It was the constant fear of his doing it that was so terrible. Sometimes when he had locked us in the room and gone away in the morning the boldest boys used to make fantastic threats of the things they would do to him when he returned, but they said them under their breath, with an eye on the door, and the rest of us quaked as we listened.

In the evenings we were marched out before him to music-halls. These music-halls were different from the ones my mother sang in. They were large rooms, with rough wooden benches and tables arranged around a square in the center, where we danced. The air was thick with tobacco smoke and heavy with the smell of ale and stout, and the ugly bearded faces of hundreds of men staring at us confused me sometimes so that I could hardly dance. I was so little, so weary from hunger and the constant fear of Mr. Hawkins, that my feet felt too heavy to lift in the hard steps, and my head swam in the glare of the lights. I wanted so much to crawl away to a quiet dark place where I could rest and feel my mother's hand tucking in the covers, that sometimes I sobbed as I danced, but I never stopped nor missed a step; I did not dare.

For all the pain and fear in my childish heart I did the steps very well, so that often the crowd cheered "the young 'un" and called for more. Then, while they shouted and banged· their mugs of ale on the tables, I would wearily dance again and again, until all my body ached. Sometimes they threw money to me, and then, after they let me go at last, Mr. Hawkins would go through my pockets for it and rap my head with his knuckles, under the suspicion that I had concealed some.

All my memory of those weeks is colored by my terror of him. It never left me. When he was in the room I got as far as possible from him and sat quite still, staring at his face and the wart on his eyelid and his great cane. When he was gone I sat and brooded about him and shivered. At the table, hungry as I was, I could not swallow my porridge under the gaze of his awful eye.

At last one night when we reached the music-hall where we were to dance we found it in great uproar. The audience was standing on benches and tables and shouting, "Slug 'im!

Slug 'im! Slug 'im!" in horrible waves of sound. In the center, where we were to dance, two men were fighting.

Mr. Hawkins pushed us before him through the crowd to a place close to them. I saw their strong naked bodies glistening under the gas flare and heard the terrible smashing blows. There was a sweetish sickening smell in the air which made me feel ill, and the roar of the crowd terrified me. Then one of the men reeled, staggered backward and fell. He was close to me and I saw his face, a shapeless mass of flesh, with no eyes, covered with blood, with blood running from the open mouth. The horror of it struck my childish mind so, after all those weeks of terror, that I fainted.

I was revived in time to dance, and the crowd, excited by the fight, threw us a great deal of money. When he searched my pockets at the door, Mr. Hawkins stooped low, put his great face almost against mine and swore, but he did not rap me with his knuckles. I was in a kind of stupor, quivering all over, and could not walk, so he put me up on his shoulder, as my father used to do, and started home.

A long time afterward I knew I was standing between his knees, while he tipped my head back and looked closely at me.

"Hingratitude, that's wot it is," he said fiercely. "Speak up, young 'un. Don't you 'ave a-plenty to eat of good 'olesome porridge? Don't you 'ave a good kind master wot never canes yer?"

"Oh, yes, sir," I said, in a panic of fear.

"Then don't you go a-being ungrateful, and a-dying on my 'ands, like young Jim done," he roared at me furiously. "You 'ear? Stubbornness, that's wot it is. I won't 'ave it!"

CHAPTER IV

In which I feel very small and desolate; encounter
once more the terrible wrath of Mr. Hawkins; and
flee from it into the unknown perils of a great
and fearful world.

"IT's stubbornness, that's wot it is! I won't
'ave it!" Mr. Hawkins said fiercely, and
reached for his cane.

I struggled in the grip of his great knees,
and cried in terror that I did not mean it, I
was sorry, I would be good. I begged him not
to beat me. Even when he let me go I could
not stop screaming.

It must have been some time next day that
I woke in a hot tumbled bed. I thought my
mother had been there, with her hair falling
over the pillow and her face all sparkling with
fun. I put up my arms with a cry, and she
was gone. A strange ugly girl, with a broom
in her hand, was leaning over me.

"Coom, coom," she said crossly, shaking my
shoulder. "Wark's to be done. No time to be
lyin' a-bed."

I struggled to get away from her heavy hand, and sobbed that I wanted my mother, I wanted to go home. I was so little and so miserable and weary that the grief of missing my mother seemed almost to break my heart.

"She's gone," the girl said, still pulling at me. "She willna be vexed wi' a girt boy, weeping like a baaby."

"No! No!" I screamed at her. "My mother hasn't gone away. My mother hasn't left me."

"Yus, she has," the girl told me. "She's gone."

I let her lift me from the bed then, and sat limp on the floor where she put me, leaning my aching head against the bedpost. All my childish courage and hope was gone, and I was left very little and alone in a terrible black world where my mother did not care for me any more. I sat there desolate, with great tears running down my cheeks, and did not wish to stir or move or ever see any one again.

Long hours later, after it had been dark a long time, Mr. Hawkins came in with the boys, and I had no strength even to fear him. When he roared at me I still sat there and only trembled and turned my head away. I remember his walking up and down and looking at me a long time, and I remember his holding a mug of ale to my lips and making me swallow some, but everything was confused and vague, and I did not care for anything, only wanting to be left alone.

It may have been the next day, or several days later, that we were all walking over rough cobbled streets, very early in the morning, in a cold thick fog. I walked unsteadily, because my legs felt limp, and Mr. Hawkins held my hand tight, so that my arm ached. We were all going to a fair in the country. I was interested in that, because my mother had once taken Sidney and me to a meadow, where we all played in the grass and found cowslips and ate cakes from a basket under a tree.

After we had walked a long time Mr. Hawkins took us into an eating-house, where we had a breakfast of sausages and I drank a big mug of hot coffee. When we came out the sun was shining and we walked down a wide white road, past many great houses with grass and trees about them. I had never imagined such places, and with the delight of seeing them, and the sunlight and the good breakfast,

I felt better, and thought I could walk by my-self if Mr. Hawkins would let go my hand, though I dared not speak of it.

As we walked on, the road grew busy with carriages coming and going and farmers' wag-ons coming in to market, and after a time a coster's cart overtook us, and Mr. Hawkins bargained with the driver to carry us.

Then I began to be almost happy again, as I sat in the back of the cart with my legs dan-gling and saw the road unrolling backward be-tween the wheels. It was a warm morning; the road was thick with white dust, and the smell of it and of the green fields, to which we came presently, and all the country sights and sounds, were pleasant. We drove for miles between the hedgerows, and I grew quite ex-cited looking for the five-barred gates in them, through which we caught glimpses of the farms on either side. So at last we came to Barnett, where the fair was to be.

The village looked bright and clean, with red brick buildings standing close to the nar-row street, and shining white cobblestones. We all climbed down before the inn, and I looked eagerly for meadows, but there were

37

none. Mr. Hawkins hurried us to the field where the fair had already begun. It was crowded with tents and people, and there was a great noise of music and shouting and cries of hokey-pokey men and venders.

"Step lively now, young 'uns," ordered Mr. Hawkins in an awful voice. " 'Ustle into them velveteen smalls, and get your jackets on in a 'urry, or I'll show you wot's wot!"

We dressed in mad haste in a little tent, and he had us into a larger one and hard at work dancing in no time. We heard his voice outside, shouting loud over the uproar of the crowd, " 'Ere! 'Ere! This way for the Lunnon clog dancers! Only a penny! See the grite Lunnon clog dancers!" A few people came in, then more, and more, till the tent was full of them, coming and going.

It was hard work dancing; my feet felt heavy to lift and my stomach ached with hunger, but I did not dare stop a minute. I danced on and on, in that hot and stuffy place, with a fearful eye on the tent-flap, where now and again Mr. Hawkins' red face appeared and glared at us, and we saw his hand with the cane gripped in it.

Over and over we did the steps, while the tent grew hotter, and laughing people came and stared and went away, until my breath came in gasps and my head swam and grew large, and larger, and then very tiny again, in a most confusing manner. Then everything went black and I must have fallen, for Mr. Hawkins was shaking me where I lay on the ground, and saying to some one, " 'E's all right. 'E's only wilful; 'e wants a good caning, 'e does."

After that I was dancing again, but I did not see the crowd any more. I only danced, and longed for the time when I might stop.

It came after a long, long while. The tent was cooler and empty when Mr. Hawkins came in and took me by the shoulder, and my head cleared so that I saw I need dance no more. My weary muscles gave way and I sat on the floor, looking at him fearfully while he wiped his face with his handkerchief.

"You, with yer woite faces!" he roared hoarsely. " 'Ow many times 'ave I told yer to look cheery while you dance? I've a mind to cane the lot of yer!" We trembled. "But I won't," he said, after a dreadful pause.

39

"We're all a-goin' hover to the inn and 'ave bread and cheese."

He took my hand again and we dragged wearily over to the inn, a bright clean place, with sawdust on the floor. It was crowded with men, and they greeted us with loud voices as we came in.

"'Ere's the Lunnon clog dancers, come to dance for bread and cheese," Mr. Hawkins said cheerfully. He looked at the barmaid, who nodded, and a place was cleared for us to begin our weary dancing again.

My tired little legs would hardly hold me up, and I stumbled in the steps. Under the terrible eye of Mr. Hawkins I did my best, panting with fear, but I could not dance. I stopped at last, and leaned against the bar. Mr. Hawkins reached for me, but as I shrank back with a cry I felt warm arms around me. It was the barmaid who held me, and after one look at her red cheeks, so close, I began to cry on her shoulder.

"Pore little dear, 'e's tired," she said, holding me tight from Mr. Hawkins. "'E shall 'ave his bread and cheese without 'is dancing."

"'E's a wilful, perverse hungrateful creetur!" Mr. Hawkins said, but she did not seem to mind. She took me behind the bar and gave me a scorching drink of something and a great piece of bread which I was too weary to eat. Afterward Mr. Hawkins took me back to the fair, jerking me furiously along by the arm. He took me to the little tent where we had dressed and put me inside.

"I'll tike the 'ide off you when I come back," he said hoarsely, bending to bring his red face close to mine. "I'll give you a caning wot *is* a caning, I will. I've been too gentle with you, I 'ave. You stay 'ere, and wait."

With these dreadful words and a horrible oath he went away, and I could hear him shouting before the other tent above the sounds of the evening's merrymaking. "'Ere! 'Ere! This way to the Lunnon clog dancers! Only a penny!"

I was left in such a state of misery and wretchedness, shaking with such fear, that not even my great weariness would let me sleep. I sat there in the dark for a long time, trembling, and then, driven by terror of Mr. Hawkins' return, I crawled beneath the edge of the tent and set out blindly to get beyond the reach of his voice.

When I came to the edge of the crowd I ran as fast as I could.

CHAPTER V

In which I have an adventure with a cow; become a
lawless filcher of brandysnaps; and confound an
honest farmer.

I RAN for a long time in the darkness, blindly,
not caring where I went, only that I escaped
from Mr. Hawkins. The pounding of my
heart shook me as I plunged across fields and
scrambled under gates in my way, until at last
I came to a corner of two hedges, and had no
strength to go farther. I curled myself into
as small a space as possible, close to the hedges,
and lay there. It seemed to me that I was
hidden and safe, and I was quite content as I
went to sleep.

Early in the morning I was awakened by
a curious swishing noise, and saw close to my
face the great staring eyes of a strange animal.
It was a cow, but I had never seen one, and I
thought it was one of the giants my mother
had told about. I saw its tongue, lapping up

43

about its nose, and as I stared it licked my face. The moist sandpapery feeling of it startled me and I howled.

At the sound it backed away with a snort, and so we remained, staring at each other for a long time. It was a bright morning, with birds singing in the hedgerows, and if it had not been for my hunger and an uneasiness lest the cow meant to lick me again I would have been quite happy, so far from Mr. Hawkins.

Then between me and the cow came a woman with a big bucket on her arm, carrying a three-legged stool. Quite fearlessly she slapped the great animal, and it turned meekly and stood, while she sat on the stool and began to milk. It was the strangest thing I had ever seen, and I went over to her side and stood watching the thin white stream pattering on the bottom of the bucket. She gave a great start and cried out in surprise when she saw me.

"Lawk a mussy!" she said, and sat with her mouth open. I must have been a strange sight in that farmyard, a thin little child—for I was only ten and very small for that age—in velveteen smalls and a round jacket with tinsel braid on it.

44

"Where did you coom from?" she asked.

"I come from London. I am an actor," I said importantly. "What are you doing?" and pointed to the bucket.

She laughed at that and seeing, I suppose, that I looked hungry, she held the bucket to my lips, and I tasted the fresh warm milk. I drank every drop, in great delight. I had never tasted anything so delicious before.

"Are you hungry?" she asked me, and I told her solemnly, believing it, that I had had nothing to eat for a week. Her consternation at that was so great she dropped the bucket, but hastily picking it up, she sat down and milked again until she had another huge draught for me. Then she finished the milking in a hurry and took me into the farmhouse kitchen, a bright place, with shining pans on the wall and a pleasant smell of cooking.

The tale I told the farmer's wife I do not remember, but she took me up in her arms, saying, "Poor little lad! Poor little lad!" over and over, while she felt my thin arms, and I squirmed, for I did not like to be pitied, and besides, I saw the breakfast on the table and wished she would let me have some. When she set me down before it at last I could hardly wait to begin, while, to my surprise, she tied a napkin around my neck.

It was a mighty breakfast—porridge and eggs, with a rasher of bacon and marmalade, and the maid who had milked the cow was cutting great slices of crusty bread and butter. But before I had taken up a spoon the farmer came in. He was a big bluff man, and at sight of me he began to ask questions in a loud voice.

"Well, my lad, where did you come from?" he said.

"From the fair, sir," I answered, eager to be at the food, and not thinking what I said.

"Oh, 'e's the little lad wi' the clog dancers I told you of, Mary," he said. "Gi' him breakfuss, if you like, and I'll be takin' him back to his master as I go to the village."

At the terrible thought of Mr. Hawkins, whom I had almost forgotten, panic took me. I sat there trembling for a second, and then, before a hand could be reached to stay me, I leaped from my chair and fled from the kitchen, through the farmyard and out the gate, the napkin fluttering at my neck. A long way down the lane I stopped, panting, and looked

to see if any one was following me. No one
was.

I wandered on for some time, growing hungrier with every step and regretting passionately the loss of that great breakfast before I
saw the girl with the brandysnaps. She was a
fat round-cheeked little girl, with her hair in
braids, and she was swinging on a gate, humming to herself and nibbling a cookie. Others
were piled on the gatepost beside her. I
stopped and looked eagerly at them and at
her. Badly as I wanted some I would not ask
for them, and she looked at me round-eyed and
said nothing.

So we eyed each other, until finally she made
a face and stuck out her tongue at me. Then
she opened her mouth wide and popped in a
brandysnap. It was too much. With a yell
I sprang at her and seized the cookies. She
tumbled from the gate, and as she fell she
howled appallingly. At the sound a great
shaggy dog came bounding, and I fled in
panic, clutching the brandysnaps.

The dog pursued me as I ran, in great leaps,
my ears filled with the fearful sound of his
barks. I sped around a turn in the lane and

47

saw before me a farmer's wagon going slowly along. The dog was hard on my heels. I caught a glimpse of his great red mouth and tongue. With a last panting effort I clambered upon the tail of the wagon and dived beneath the burlap which covered the load.

There, lying in the dimness among green vegetables, I consumed the brandysnaps to the last crumb, listening to the farmer's bewildered expostulation with the honest dog, which continued barking at the wagon until the farmer dismounted and pursued him down the road with his whip. Then, as the wagon went onward again, I ate a number of radishes and a raw potato, and experimentally bit the squash and marrows until, with a contented stomach, I curled up among the lettuce and fell asleep.

I was awakened by the stopping of the wagon and heard the farmer, busied with the horse, exchanging jovial greetings with other gruff voices. Undecided what to do, I lay still until I heard him speaking loudly almost over my head.

"I lay these are the finest vegetables ever come to market," he said proudly, and tore the burlap covering from me. I sat up.

48

There never was a more surprised farmer. He stood open-mouthed. While the men around him laughed, I scrambled from among the vegetables over the wagon's edge and dived into the uproar of Covent Garden market. Horses, donkeys, wagons, men, women and children crowded the place; on every side were piles of vegetables and bright fruit, and there was a clamor of laughter, shouts and the cries of hucksters.

I ran about, happy in all the confusion, and glad to feel London about me again. After a while I met a man who gave me a penny for helping him unload his vegetables, and I wandered out of the market and down the dirty cobbled streets outside. There was a barrel organ which I followed for a time, and then I met a hokey-pokey man and spent my penny for his sweets. I felt as rich as a lord as I sat on the curb in the sunshine eating them.

CHAPTER VI

In which I come home again; accustom myself to
going to bed hungry; and have an unexpected encounter with my father.

As I sat there in the sunshine eating the hokey-
pokey for which I had spent my only penny
all my old dreams came back to me. I imagined myself rich and famous, bowing before
cheering audiences, wearing a tall silk hat and
a cane, and buying my mother a silk dress.

It was a rough dirty street, swarming with
ragged children and full of heavy vans driven
by swearing drivers, but reality did not inter-
fere with my dreams. It never has.

When I had licked the last sweetness of the
cream from my fingers I rose and walked with
a haughty swagger, raising my eyebrows dis-
dainfully. It was difficult to look down on
a person whose waistband was on a level with
my eyes, but I managed it. Then I amused
myself walking behind people and imitating
them, until I heard a barrel organ and followed
it, dancing with the other children.

I was adventurous and gay that morning,

with no cares in the world. What did it matter that I had no food nor shelter nor friends in all London? I did not think of that.

It was late that afternoon, and I had wandered a long way, when my increasing hunger began to damp my spirits. My feet dragged before the windows of pastry shops, and the fruit on the street stands tempted me. When it grew dark and the gas lamps were lighted I felt very little and lonely again and longed to cry. The streets were crowded with people hurrying home—women with market baskets, and rough men, but no one noticed me. I was only a ragged hungry child, and there are thousands of them in London.

At last I stood forlorn before a baker's window looking at the cakes and buns inside and wanting them with all my heart. I stood there a long time, jostled by people going by, till a woman stopped beside me to look in also. Something about her skirt and shoes gave me a wild hope, and I looked up. It was my mother. My mother!

I clasped her about the knees and screamed. Then I felt her arms tight about me and she was kneeling beside me while we sobbed together. My mother, my dear mother, at last. She had not gone away; she had not forgotten me; she wanted me as much as ever. I clutched her, shaking and sobbing, as if I could never let go, until, little as she was, she picked me up and carried me home.

She was not living in actors' lodgings any more; she had a poor little room in Palermo Terrace, Kensington—a room little better than the dreadful one where Mr. Hawkins had kept me—but it was like Heaven to me to be there, with my mother. I clung to her a long time, hysterical when she tried to take my arms from her neck, and we laughed and cried together while she petted and comforted me.

Neither my father nor Sidney was there, nor was there any sign that they were expected. When I was quieter, sitting on her lap eating a bun and tea, my mother said that they were gone. On the day I ran away with Mr. Hawkins, Sidney had gone to sea. My mother had a note from him, telling her about his grand place as steward's assistant on a boat going to Africa, and promising to bring her back beautiful presents and money. She had not heard from him again.

She undressed me with her tiny hands that
reminded me of birds' claws and tucked me
in bed, just as I had dreamed so often, with
her soft hair falling over the pillow, and I
went to sleep, my heart almost bursting with
happiness at being home again.

When I woke in the morning, so early that
it was not yet light, I saw her sitting beside a
lamp, sewing. All my memories of my mother
for weeks after that are pictures of her sitting
sewing, her sweet thin face, with dark circles
under the eyes, bending over the work and her
fingers flying. She was making blouses for
a factory. There were always piles of them,
finished and unfinished, on the table and bed,
and she never stopped work on them. When
I awoke in the night I saw her in the lamp-
light working, and all day long she worked,
barely stopping to eat. When she had a great
pile of them finished I took them to the factory
and brought back more for her to do.

I used to climb the long dark stairs to the
factory loft with the bundle and watch the
man who took the blouses and examined them,
hating him. He was a sleek fat man, with
rings on his fingers, and he used to point out

every stitch which was not just right, and claim there were spots on the blouses, though there were none at all, and then he kept out some of the money. My mother got half a crown —about fifty cents—for a dozen blouses, and by working all week without stopping a minute she earned about five shillings.

I would keep out three and six for the rent money, and then go bargaining at the market stalls for food. A pound of two-penny bits of meat, with a pennyworth of pot-herbs, made us a stew, and sometimes I got a bit of stale bread besides. Then I came panting up the stairs to my mother with the bundles, and gave her the rent money, warm from being clutched in my hand, and she would laugh and kiss me and say how well I had done.

The stew had to last us the week, and I know now that often my mother made only a pretense of eating, so that there would be more for me. I was always hungry in those days and used to dream of cakes and buns, but we were very happy together. Sometimes I would do an errand for some one and get a penny, and then I proudly brought it to her and we would have buns, or even a herring, for supper.

54

But she was uneasy when I was away, and wanted me to sit by her and read aloud while she worked, so I did not often leave her.

At this time she was passionately eager to have me study. She had taught me to read before, and now while she sewed she talked to me about history and other countries and peoples, and showed me how to draw maps of the world, and we played little spelling games. She had me read the Bible aloud to her for hours at a time. It was the only book we had. But most of all she taught me acting. I had a great gift for mimicry, and she had me mimic every one I saw in the streets. I loved it and used to make up little plays and act them for her.

Remembering the first time I had danced on the stage, and the money I made, I wanted to go back to the music-halls, but she roused almost into a fury at the idea. All her most painful memories were of the music-hall life, and she passionately made me promise never to act in one. I could not have done it in any case, because at this time there was a law forbidding children under fourteen to work on the stage. I was only eleven.

55

My mother grew thinner and more tired. She complained sometimes of a pain in her head, and her beautiful hair, like long, fine silk, had threads in it that shone like silver. I loved to watch them when she brushed it at night. But she was always gay and sweet with me, and I adored her. I had no life at all separate from her; all my dreams and hopes were of making her happy and buying her beautiful things, and taking her to a place in the country where she could rest and do nothing but play with me.

Then one day while I was coming from the factory with the money clutched in my hand I passed a barroom. I had never been in one, or cared to, but something seemed to attract me to this one. I stood before the swinging doors, thinking with a fluttering heart of going in, and wanting to, and not wanting to, both at once. Finally I timidly pushed the doors apart and looked in. There, at a little table, drinking with some men, I saw my father.

CHAPTER VII

In which I see my father for the last time; learn
that real tragedy is silent; and go out into the
world to make my own way.

IT gave me a great shock to recognize my
father in the man who sat there drinking. I
quivered as I looked at him. He was changed;
his dark handsome face had reddened and
looked swollen and flabby; his eyes were blood-
shot. He did not see me at first. The man
with him appeared to be urging something,
and my father cried with an oath that he would
not. I caught the word "hospital," and saw
his hands shake as he pounded the table. Then
some one coming in pushed me into the room
and he saw me.

"Hello, here's the little tike!" he cried.
"Blast me, he hasn't grown an inch! Here,
come here to your daddy!"

I went over to the table and stood looking
at him, the bundles under my arm. He was
very boisterous, calling all the men in the bar
to see me, and boasting of how I could dance.

He swung me to the table-top, crying, "Come, my beauty, show 'em what you can do!" and they began to clap. I danced for them, and then I mimicked them one by one until the room was in an uproar.

"He's his father's own son!" they cried. "Little Charlie Chaplin!"

My father was very proud of me and kept me at it until I was tired, and, remembering that my mother was waiting, I climbed down from the table and picked up my bundles.

"Going without a drink?" cried my father, and offered me his glass, but I pushed it away. I did not like the smell of it. My father seemed hurt and angry; he drained the glass and put it on the table with a slam, and I saw again how his hand shook.

"Just like his mother!" he said bitterly. "Despises his own father! I'm not good enough for his little highness. She's taught him that."

"It's not true!" I cried, enraged. "My mother never says a word about you!"

"Oh, don't she?" he sneered, but his lip shook. He stared moodily at the table, drumming on it with his fingers, and then he turned to me with a dreary look in his eyes. "Well, then, come home with me," he said. "I'll take good care of you and give you a fine start in the profession and clothes that aren't rags. I can do that, yet. I'm not done for, whatever they say. Come, will you do it?"

"No," I said. "I want to stay with my mother."

"We'll see about that!" he shouted angrily. He seized my arm and shook it. "You'll come with me, if I say so. You hear?" He glared at me and I looked back at him, frightened.

"You hurt! I want to go home to my mother!" I cried.

He held me a minute and then wearily pushed me away. "All right, go and be damned!" he said. "It's a hell of a life." Then, with a sudden motion, he caught my hand and put a sovereign in it. I dodged through the crowd and escaped into the street, eager to take the money to my mother.

The next week, as we were sitting together, my mother sewing and I painfully spelling out long words in my reading, the landlady came puffing up the stairs and knocked at the door.

"Your mister's took bad and in the hospital,"

59

she said to my mother. "He's sent a message 'e wants to see you."

My mother turned whiter and rose in a hurry to put on her bonnet, while I picked the bits of thread from her gown. Then she kissed me, told me to mind the stew and not go out till she came back, and went away.

There seemed a horror left in the room when she was gone. I could not keep my thoughts from that word "hospital," which all the poor of London fear and dread. I wandered about the room, looking from the window at the starving cats in the court and at the brick wall opposite till it grew dark. Then I ate a small plate of the stew, leaving some for my mother, and went miserably to bed.

Late in the night my mother woke me and I saw that her face was shining almost as it used to do.

"Oh, my dear!" she cried, hugging me. "It's all right. We are going to be so happy again!" She rocked back and forth, hugging me, and her hair tumbled down about us. Then she told me that when my father was well we were all going to leave London and go far away together—to Australia. We were going to have a farm there, in the country, with cows, and I was to have milk and cream and eggs, and she would make butter, and my father would never drink again. She poured it all out, in little bursts of talk, and her warm tears fell on my face.

When at last she left me to brush out her hair she hummed a little song and smiled at herself in the tiny mirror.

"I wish my hair was all brown as it used to be," she said. "It hurt him so to see it white. I will get fat in the country. Do you remember how handsome your father was and how jolly? Oh, won't it be fun?" After she had put out the light we lay a long time in the dark talking, and she told me tales of the pleasant times they had when I was little and asked if I remembered them.

After that my mother went every day to the hospital. She did not sew any more, and she bought bunches of flowers and fruit for my father and cakes for me. At night, when she tucked me in, her face was bright with hope, and hearing her laugh, I remembered how seldom she had done it lately. We were both very happy.

61

Then one day she came in slowly, stumbling a bit. My heart gave a terrible leap when I saw her face—gray, with a blue look about her lips. I ran to her, frightened, and helped her to a chair. She sat there quite still, not answering me at first, and then she said in a dull voice, "He's dead. He's dead. He was dead when I got there. It can't be true. He's dead."

My father had died suddenly the night before. There was some confusion about the burial arrangements. My mother seemed dazed and there was no money. People came and talked with her and she did not seem to understand them, but it seemed that the music-hall people were making the arrangements, and then that somebody objected to that and undertook them—I gathered that it was my father's sister.

Then one day my mother and I dressed very carefully and went to the funeral. It was a foggy cold day, late in autumn, with drops of rain falling slowly. At one end of the grave stood a thin angular woman with her lips pressed together tight, and my mother and I stood at the other. My mother held her head proudly and did not shed a tear, but her hand in mine was cold. There were several carriages and people from the music-halls with a few flowers. When the coffin was lowered into the grave the thin hard-looking woman dropped some flowers on it. My mother looked at her and she looked at my mother coldly. We had no flowers, but my mother took from my pocket a little handkerchief of hers which she had given me—a little handkerchief with an embroidered border which I prized very much—and put it in my hand.

"You can put that in," she said, and I dropped it into the open grave and watched it flutter down. My heart was almost breaking with grief for my mother.

Then we went back to our cold room alone, and my mother went at once at her sewing.

We had no more talks or study, and she did not seem to hear when I read aloud, so after a time I stopped. She sat silently, all day, sewing at the blouses, and I hunted for errands in the streets, and made the stew, and tried to get her to eat some. She said she did not care to eat because her head ached, she would rather I had it.

At this time I looked everywhere for work,

but could not seem to find any. I was so small and thin that people thought I could not do it well. I picked up a few pennies here and there and learned the ways of the streets, and wished I were bigger and not so shabby, so that I might go on the stage. I was sure I could make money there.

Then one day I came home and found my mother lying on the floor beside her chair, gray and cold, with blue lips. I could not rouse her. I screamed on the staircase for the landlady, and she came up and we worked over my mother together. After a while the parish doctor came—a busy bustling little man. He pursed up his lips and shook his head. "Infirmary case!" he said briskly. "Looks bad!"

A wagon came and they took my mother away, still gray and cold. She had not moved or spoken to me. When she had gone I sat at the top of the staircase in blank hopeless misery, thinking of the grave in which they had buried my father, and that I would never see my mother again. After a while the landlady came up with a broom.

"Well, well," she said crossly. "I 'ave my room to let again. It's a 'ard world. I'm a poor woman, you know; you can't stay 'ere."

"Yes, I know. I have other lodgings," I said importantly, so that she should not see how miserable I was. I went into the room with her and looked around. I had nothing to take away but a comb and a collar. I put them in my pocket and left.

When I was on the stairs the landlady called to me from the top.

"You know I'd like to keep you 'ere if I could," she said.

"Yes, I know. But I can look out for myself," I said. I put my hands in my pockets and whistled to show her I needed no pity, and went out into the street.

CHAPTER VIII

In which I take lodgings in a barrel and find that I have invaded a home; learn something about crime; and forget that I was to share in nefarious profits.

IT was a cold wet evening in the beginning of winter and the rain struck chilly through my thin clothes as I walked, wondering where I could find shelter. Probably in America a homeless, hungry child of eleven would find friends, but in London I was only one of thousands as wretched as I. Such poverty is so common there that people are accustomed to it and pass by with their minds full of their own concerns.

I wandered aimlessly about for a long time, watching the gas lamps flare feebly, one by one, and make long, glimmering marks on the wet pavements. I could not whistle any more, there was such an ache in my throat at the thought of my mother, and I was so miserable and forlorn. At last I found an overturned barrel with a little damp straw in it in an alley, and I curled up in it and lay there hearing the raindrops muffled, hollow, beating above me.

After a while I must have fallen into a dose, for I was awakened by something crawling into the barrel. I thought it was a dog and put out my hand, half afraid and half glad of the company. It was another boy.

"Hello, 'ere!" he said. "Wot are you up to? This 'ere is *my* 'ome!"

"I don't care, I'm here and I'm going to stay here," I said. "Say what you like about that!"

"Ho, you are, are you? I'll punch your bloomin' 'ead off first!" he answered.

"I won't go, not for twenty punchings," I said doggedly. There was not room to fight in the barrel and I was sure he could not get me out, because I knew by the feel of his wet shoulder in the dark that he was smaller than I.

"'Ere's a pretty go, a man carn't 'ave 'is own 'ome!" he said bitterly, after we had sat breathing hard for a minute. "Wot's yer name?"

I told him who I was and how I had come there and promised to leave in the morning. He was much interested in hearing that I had a mother and asked what she was like, assuming at once a condescending air. He had never had a mother, he said importantly; he knew his way about, he did.

"You can stye 'ere if you like," he said grandly. "'Ave you 'ad grub?"

I told him no, that I had not been able to find anything to eat.

"Hi know, the cats get to it first," he said. "But hi 'ave my wye, hi 'ave. 'Ere's 'arf a bun for yer." He put into my hand a damp bit of bread and I ate it gratefully while he talked. His name was Snooper, he said, and he could show me about—how to snatch purses and dodge the bobbies and have larks.

At last we went to sleep, curled in the damp straw, with an understanding that the next day we should forage together for purses. Next morning I was awakened by a terrific noise, and crawling from the barrel found Snooper standing outside kicking it. He was a wizened, small child, not more than nine years old, wearing a ragged coat too small for him and a man's trousers torn off at the knee. He. wore his cap on one side with a jaunty air and whistled, his hands in the rents in his coat.

68

We started off together to Covent Garden market, where he said we would find good pickings, and seeing the knowing cock of his eye and his gay manner, I too managed to whistle and walk with a swagger, though my heart was still heavy with missing my mother, and I was very hungry. It was early when we came to the market, but the place was crowded with farmers' wagons and horses and costers' carts. We wandered about and Snooper, with great enterprise, filled the front of his blouse with raw eggs, which we ate in a near-by alley. When we returned to the market it was beginning to fill with purchasers. Snooper, with his finger at his nose and a cock of his eye, pointed out one of them, a fat woman in black, carrying a big market basket on her arm and clutching a fat leather purse.

"When I glom the leather you hupset the heggs at 'er feet," he said to me in a hoarse whisper, and we edged closer to her through the crowd. She was standing before a vegetable stand with a bunch of herbs in her hand arguing with the farmer.

"Thrippence," said the farmer firmly.

"Tuppence ha'penny, not a farthing more,"

she said. "It's robbery, that's wot it is." We edged closer.

"Worth fourpence by rights," said the farmer. "Take 'em for thrippence or leave 'em."

"Tuppence ha'penny," she insisted. "They're stale. Tuppence ha'—ow!" Snooper had snatched her purse.

With a yell she leaped after him, stumbled and fell in the crate of eggs. The farmer, rushing from behind his stand, overturned the pumpkins, which bounced among the crowd. There was great uproar. I fled.

Diving under wagons and dodging among the horses and people, I had gone half-way down the big market when I encountered a perspiring, swearing farmer, who was trying to unload his wagon and hold his horse at the same time. The beast was plunging and rearing.

"Hi, lad!" the farmer called to me. "Want a ha'penny? 'Old 'is bloomin' 'ead for me and I'll gi' you one."

I gladly seized the halter, and a few minutes later I had the halfpenny and a carrot as well. I liked the market, with all its noise and bustle

70

and the excitement of seeing new things, and while I wandered through the crowd munching my carrot I decided to stay there. Snooper had said he would wait for me at the barrel and divide the contents of the purse, but among all the interesting sights and sounds of the market I forgot that, and although I looked for him several days later, I never saw him again.

Before noon I had earned another ha'penny and an apple, only partly spoiled. I had not eaten an apple since the old days when I was very little and mother used to bring home treats to Sidney and me. The loneliness of my mother still lay at the bottom of my heart like a dull ache, and I determined to take the apple to her. The parish doctor who had taken her away had said I might be able to see her at the hospital that afternoon.

I held the apple carefully all the long way through the London streets to the hospital. It was a big bare place, with very busy people coming and going, and for a long time I could not get any one to tell me where my mother was. At last a woman all in black, with a wide, flaring white cap on her head, took my hand and led me past a great many beds with moaning people in them to the one where my mother lay.

They had cut away all her beautiful hair, and her small bare head looked strange upon the pillow. Her eyes were wide open and bright, but they frightened me, and though she was talking rapidly to herself, she did not say a word to me when I stood beside her and showed her the apple.

"Mother, mother, see, I've brought you something," I said, but she only turned her head restlessly on the pillow.

"One more. Are the bottonholes finished? Nine more to make the dozen, and then a dozen more, and that's a half-crown, and thread costs so much," she went on to herself.

"What's the matter with my mother? Why don't she speak to me?" I asked the woman in the white cap.

"It's the fever—she's out of her head, poor thing," the woman said.

"Won't she ever be able to speak to me?" I asked her, and something in the way she shook her head and said she didn't know made me cold all over. Then she led me out again and I went back to Covent Garden market.

CHAPTER IX

In which I trick a Covent Garden coster; get glorious news from Sidney; and make another sad trip to the hospital.

I SLEPT that night in Covent Garden market, cuddled close to the back of a coster's donkey, which was warm, but caused me great alarm at intervals by wheezing loudly and making as if to turn over upon me. Then I scurried out of the straw and wandered about in the empty, echoing place, feeling very small in the vast dimness among the shadows, until the donkey was quiet again and I could creep back beside him.

In the strange eery chill of the morning, while the gas lamps in the streets were still showing dimly through in the fog, the farmers began to come in with their wagons. I hurried about in the darkness of the market, asking each one if I might help him unload the vegetables or hold the horse for a halfpenny,

73

or even for a carrot or raw potato. The horses were large, heavy-footed beasts and their broad, huge-muscled chests towered over me as I held the halters, while every toss of their heads lifted me from the floor. But I held on bravely, very hungry, thinking of the bun I might buy with a halfpenny, and indeed, before the market was light I had two halfpennies and a small assortment of vegetables.

I ate these, and then I went out into the dirty, cobbled streets about the market where the heavy vans were already beginning to rumble by and found an eating-house where, for my penny, I bought not only two buns, but a big mug of very hot coffee as well. As I sat on a stool drinking and taking bites from the buns, the waiter leaned his elbows on the counter and asked me where I had come from and who I was.

"I am an actor," I told him, for this idea was always in the back of my mind. He laughed heartily at this, and I swallowed the rest of the coffee in a hurry, scalding my throat, for I resented his laughing and wished to get away. I put the bits of bun in my pocket and slipped down from the stool, but before I

74

had reached the door the man came around the counter with another bun in his hand.

" 'Ere, me pore lad, tike this," he said kindly enough, putting the bun in my pocket. I let him do it, feeling confused and resentful, and ate the bun later, sitting on a box in the market, but I never went back to that eating-house again. I hated to be pitied.

All the months I lived in Covent Garden market I was hungry. I ate eagerly every bit of spoiled fruit or partly decayed vegetable I could find, and sometimes the farmers, amused by my dancing for them while they were eating, would give me crusts from their baskets, but my stomach was never satisfied. The people who came to Covent Garden market were poor, and halfpennies were scarce, though I hunted all day long for small jobs that I could do. Very early in the morning when the farmers first came in was the best time to find them, but sometimes days went by when all I could earn was raw vegetables.

After a time, when the market people knew me, I had permission to sleep in one of the coster's carts, with a sack over me for warmth, but at first I curled up in the straw beside the donkeys. One of the donkeys in particular was quite sleek and fat. His owner took great pride in him, feeding him every day a large portion of carrots, and fondly swearing at him while he ate them. I used to look enviously at that donkey and finally I evolved a great plan.

When the donkey had first begun to munch the carrots, I would scream from the tail of the cart, "Thieves! Thieves! Catch 'im!" and spring away, overturning boxes and making a great commotion. The coster would leave his donkey and come running, excited, and while he was wondering what had happened I would steal slyly up on the other side of the donkey and filch the carrots. The poor beast looked reproachfully at me, wagging his ears and sometimes braying frightfully, but I ran gleefully away, and sitting concealed beneath a wagon, ate his dinner for him to the last bite.

The stupid coster, amazed, would scratch his head and marvel at the donkey's appetite, but I do not remember that he ever failed to run at the cry of "Thieves!" or that I ever failed to make way with the carrots.

Several times that winter I screwed up my

courage to attempt getting work on the stage, but after I had walked a long way in the foggy, dripping streets, I would be so cold and wet and so conscious of my rags and of my dirty collar that I turned back to the market again.

Sometimes at long intervals the people at the hospital let me see my mother, but I could not bear to look at her, she was so altered and seemed so strange. She lay quite still, sometimes, and would not speak or answer me when I called to her, so that I thought she was dead, and a great black misery came over me. Sometimes she turned her head from side to side on the pillow and talked to herself in a quick, clear voice about blouses, dozens and dozens of blouses. She never looked at me or seemed to know that I was there, and I came away from the hospital so wretched that I wished never to go back.

Still I went again, as often as they would let me, and one day a marvelous thing happened. The nurse with the flaring white cap took me into a little office and showed me a letter.

"A woman brought it here from the lodgings where your mother lived," she said. "We read it to your mother, but she could not understand, so we saved it for you."

She gave it to me and I read it in great excitement. .

"Dear mother," it read. "I am coming back from Africa. I will be home for Christmas Day, with thirty pounds saved, and I am bringing grand presents for you, but I will not tell you what they are. Tell Charlie to look out for his big brother, I have presents for him, too. I will be home two months from to-day, at Waterloo station at nine o'clock. Be sure to have a Christmas pudding ready. Hoping you are all well, I am your dutiful son,
                              "Sidney.
"Postscript—It is a shawl, and there are earrings, too, but I will not tell you what else."

My heart gave a great leap and seemed to choke me, and I trembled so I could not speak. I had not thought of Sidney for a long time, and now he was coming home with money and presents! And thinking of my poor mother, who was so ill and could not understand the great news, tears came into my eyes so that I had to rub them not to let the nurse see. Then

78

I saw how dirty I was, and ragged, and was ashamed to have Sidney see me.

The nurse kindly told the day, and comparing it with the date of the letter, I saw it was that very evening that Sidney would reach London.

Quivering with excitement, I begged to see my mother again and tell her about it, and when they said I might, I could not walk down the long ward, but must run in my eagerness. "Mother! Mother! Sidney's coming home! With presents for you—a shawl, and earrings!" I cried. But it was no use. My mother lay there with her thin drawn face quite still and would not even open her eyes.

So, with a heavy heart, wondering how I was to tell Sidney of all that had occurred, I came out of the hospital and tried to make ready for going to Waterloo station.

I washed my face and hands carefully in a puddle and dried them upon some straw. Then I took some mud and blacked my shoes as well as possible, and the toe which showed so that it would not be so conspicuous. Then my hands must be washed again and my hair combed. I smoothed out my wrinkled clothes as well as I could and tucked in the torn lining of my cap so that it would not show.

All this took much time, so that it was almost dusk before I started to meet Sidney, and I ran most of the way, not to be late, hoping that I would not miss him in all the confusion of the station.

CHAPTER X

In which Sidney comes home to find father dead, mother too ill to recognize him and me half starved and in rags.

WHEN at last I arrived, panting, at Waterloo station the lamps were already lighted and all the place was bright with them. There was such a noise of people coming and going and so much confusion that, used as I was to the turmoil of the market, I hardly knew where to go or what to do. Besides, the manner of these people was so different and their clothes so good that I felt more than ever ashamed of my raggedness and doubtful what Sidney would think when he saw me.

However, I was so determined not to miss him that I got up courage to ask the way to the trains and was waiting there trembling with excitement and eagerness when the nine o'clock express came in. I had not quite courage enough to run forward, but hung back a little, keeping my broken shoe with the hole in it where my toe showed behind the other and looking carefully at each man that passed in the hope that he might be Sidney.

At last I saw him. He was almost seventeen then; big, well-dressed and healthy looking as he swung along with his cap pushed back looking eagerly at every woman in sight, expecting, I knew, to see my mother. He went by me without a glance and I saw his bright clean boots and the new glove he wore on the hand that held his bag. They seemed to put such a distance between us that I let him go past, not daring to stop him. I stood there stupidly looking at his back.

Then I realized that he was going, that I was losing him, and I ran after him and desperately touched his arm. He looked down at me impatiently.

"No, lad," he said sharply, "I will carry the bag."

He went on through the station still watching for my mother, and I followed him, ashamed to speak to him again, ragged and dirty as I was, and yet not being able to let him go. At last he gave up hope of my mother's coming to meet him and went outside, where he hailed a cab. I stood there beside him trying to speak to him and choking while the driver opened the cab door and he got in. Then I could bear it no longer. I seized the door handle and clung to it desperately.

"Oh, Sidney, don't you know me?" I cried. "I'm Charlie."

He looked at me a minute, surprised, before he recognized me. Then his face went white and he pulled me into the cab, calling to the driver to go on, anywhere.

"For God's sake, what has happened?" he asked.

"Father's dead and mother's in the parish hospital, and I haven't had anywhere to sleep or to wash," I blurted out.

Sidney did not speak for a minute. His face seemed to set and harden as I watched it, while the cab bumped over the cobbles.

"How long has this been going on?" he said at last, choking over the words.

"About three months," I said. Then I told him as much as I could, tangling it up because there was so much to say—about father's death. and how my mother had sewed, and why I was so dirty because I had no soap and had to sleep

83

in the cart, and that I could not make mother understand that his letter had come.

"And I've been—saving my money!" he said, once, like a groan, and his hand shook. Then he became very brisk and spoke sharply ' to the driver, ordering him where to go.

I sat in the cab while he got out to see about rooms and then he came back and took me into a place that seemed as beautiful as a palace— a suite of rooms with lace curtains, and carpets, and a piano, and a fireplace. I stood on some papers and undressed, while Sidney drew the bath for me, and it seemed as unreal as a fairy tale.

"Good heavens, you're starving!" Sidney cried when he saw how thin I was, and he sent out for hot milk and biscuits. Then, leaving me happy with the hot water and soap and plenty of clean soft towels, he went out, taking my rags done in a bundle.

When he came back I was sitting wrapped in his bathrobe, curling my toes before the fire, as happy as I could possibly be. He brought new clothes for me, warm underwear and a Norfolk suit and new shoes. When I was dressed in them, with my hair combed and a bright silk tie knotted under a clean white collar, I walked up and down, feeling cocky enough to speak to a king, except when I saw Sidney's white set face and thought of my poor mother.

"I got a permit to see her to-night," Sidney said. "I have the cab waiting. I thought maybe when she saw the presents I brought— and saw you looking so well—she always liked you best—"

So we set out in the cab again for the hospital. I felt quite grand coming up the steps in my new clothes and walked among the nurses, who did not recognize me at first, with a superior air, speaking to them confidently. I led Sidney down the long ward I knew so well, holding my head high, but all my new importance left me when I saw my mother.

She lay there with her eyes closed and her sweet face so thin, with deep hollows in the cheeks and dark marks under her lashes, that the old fear hurt my heart and I trembled.

"Is she—is she alive?" I asked the nurse.

"Yes. Speak to her and rouse her if you can," she said. Sidney and I leaned over the bed and called to her.

"Mother, look! Here's Sidney home! Look, mother!" I said cheerily.

"See, mother dear—all the beautiful presents. Wake up and see—it's Christmas!" Sidney said, taking her hand. She did not seem to hear at first, and then she turned her head on the pillow and opened her eyes.

"Here we are, mother!" we cried happily. "All the hard times are over—we'll have Christmas together—look at the lovely things Sidney's brought—see Charlie's new clothes." We tumbled the words together, excited and eager.

"Is—it—morning?" mother said painfully. "Three dozen more to sew. He shouldn't keep out the money for spots, there were no spots at all. Twelve make a dozen, and that's a half-crown, and then a dozen more, and then a dozen more, and then a dozen more—" She did not know us at all.

Sidney spread over the bed the beautiful shawl he had brought for her and put the earrings in her hand and showed her the comb of brilliants for her hair, which the nurses had cut away, but she only turned her head restlessly on the pillow and talked wildly until the nurse told us we must come away.

We rode back to the rooms, not saying a word. Sidney sat with his arm about my shoulders and his eyes were hard and bright. When we were home again he ordered up a great supper of chops and a meat pie and pudding. We sat down and he piled my plate high with food. Then suddenly he put his arms down on the table and began to sob.

It was terrible. He could not stop. I tried to speak to him, but could not, so after a moment I got up and went over to the window. I stood there leaning my forehead against the glass, looking at the lights outside, so miserable that I could not cry. What was the good of all this comfort without our mother?

Sidney came over after a while and we stood together not saying anything for a long time. Then he drew a deep breath and said: "Well, all we can do is to go on. I suppose we must look up a berth for you after you have been fed up a bit. What do you want to do?"

"I want to be an actor," I answered dully.

"All right. We'll see what we can do to-morrow," he said.

CHAPTER XI

In which I vainly make the rounds of the theatrical agents; almost go to sea; and at last get the chance for which I have long been yearning.

NOTHING, I believe, makes so much difference, not only with the appearance of a man, but with the man himself, as good clothes and a well-filled stomach, and this is even more true of a boy, who is more sensitive to impressions of every sort.

When I was dressed next morning in my new clothes, which already had almost ceased to feel strange to me, and had eaten a breakfast so large that Sidney's eyes widened with alarm while he watched me, I did not feel at all like the shabby boy of the day before. I did a few dance steps, in high spirits, and mimicked for Sidney's benefit a great many of the market people and the coster who had fed his donkey carrots. I even assumed a little of my old patronizing attitude toward Sidney, who had

88

never been considered the clever one of the family, and promised him large returns for all he had done for me as soon as I should become a famous actor.

This matter of cleverness I believe now to be greatly overrated. The clever person is too apt to let his cleverness excuse the absence of most of the solid qualities of character, and to rely on facility and surface brilliance to supply the want of industry and prudence. All my life I have been going up like a rocket, all sparks and a loud noise, and coming down like one again, but Sidney has always been the steady stand-by of the family, ready to pick me out of the mud and start me up again. He is the better man of the two.

That morning, though, after I had eaten his breakfast, I could not imagine myself ever in need of help again and my mind was full of future success on the stage. I could hardly wait while he dressed to go with me to the agents, and when we were in the streets I walked with a swagger, and pointed out the sights as if he were only a provincial and I at least a capitalist of London.

I was just twelve then and the law was strict

89

against the employment on the stage of children under fourteen, but I do not remember that I ever had any difficulty in convincing the agents that I was over the legal age. My self-confidence and my talent for mimicry were so strong that they overcame the impression of my small size, and I suppose the month of hunger and suffering for my mother had given my face an older look.

In the weeks which followed Sidney's home-coming we visited dozens of agents. I climbed the long stairs to their offices in a fever of expectation and hope; I talked to each agent quite confidently, and when he had taken my name and address and said he had nothing for me at present, I came down again in the depths of gloom, so despondent that only a good dinner and a visit to the theater would cheer me. I always felt that I could play the parts much better than any actor I saw, and so I came away in high spirits again.

Every day we went to see my mother, and the nurses said she was a little better, but she never knew us or spoke to us and we could not see any change. This sadness because she could not be happy with us made our rooms seem gloomy when we returned to them, and I know that Sidney felt it always. Often, planning what we should do when she was well again, and how proud she would be of my success when I was a great actor, I almost believed it all true and was as happy as if it were. My imagination has always seemed truer to me than facts.

Christmas came and went and I did not have an offer of a place on the stage. Sidney must go back to sea. Nearly all of his savings were gone and he felt he must leave some money to buy little delicacies for my mother. The problem of what to do with me bothered him, and when he spoke of it, as he did sometimes, all my dreams faded suddenly and I felt so desolate that if I had been smaller I would have wept in despair.

At last he arranged with his company to take me on the ship as cabin-boy. He said it would not be half bad, I might grow to like the sea, and although I hated the thought of it, it seemed better than going back to Covent Garden market again. We were to sail sometime in January, bound for Africa. As a last resort we made the rounds of the theatrical agents

91

again, but there was nothing in sight for me, and so it was settled that I must go to sea.

Sidney bought me a little bag and packed it with the things I should need on ship-board. We gave up the lodgings and paid a last visit to mother. This time she was quieter and looked at us several times almost as if she recognized us. It nearly broke my heart to leave her so, but we could not think of anything else to do.

The morning of our last day in London my breakfast almost choked me. Our bags were packed, waiting beside our chairs, and it seemed to me that everything in the world was wrong. I knew I should not like the sea. The maid had brought in a few letters, with the bill for the lodgings, and Sidney was looking them over. Suddenly he looked at me queerly and threw a card across the table to me.

"Seems to be for you," he said. I turned it over in a hurry and read it. It said, "Call and see me, Frank Stern, 55 the Strand." Frank Stern was a theatrical agent.

I leaped from my chair with a shout of excitement.

"What price the sea now?" I cried. "I've

got a place worth the whole of it! Where's my hat?"

"Go slow, go slow, lad," said Sidney. "You haven't got the place yet, you know."

"I've as good as got it," I retorted, tearing open the bags to find my comb and a clothes brush. "Come, now, Sidney, lend me your cane? An actor has to have a cane, you know."

Sidney lent me his cane, and I leaped down the stairs three steps at a time.

A tram would not do, I must have a cab to go in a style suiting my new position. All the way I gave myself the airs of a great actor, looking haughtily from the cab-window at the common Londoners and thinking how the audiences would applaud when I strode down the stage.

Frank Stern was a little man, plump and important, with a big diamond on his finger, and he began by clearing his throat in an impressive manner and looking me over very sharply, but I sat down with a careless air, swinging Sidney's cane and asked him in an offhand way if he had anything particularly good. At the moment so great was the power of my imaginings on my own mind I felt quite careless as to whether I got the place or not and was resolved not to take any small part unworthy my talents.

"It's the leading part with a provincial company *From Rags to Riches*," he said. "Our lead's fallen sick and we need a new one in a hurry. Think you can do it?"

"E—Er—provincial company," I said doubtfully. "I had not thought of leaving London. Still—what's the screw?"

"One pound ten a week," he answered.

"Impossible!" I said. "I could not think of it."

"Well—we might make it two pounds. We need some one in a hurry. If you are a quick study and make a good showing at rehearsal— say two pounds. Yes, I'll make it two pounds."

"It's a small salary—a very small salary," I said gruffly. I, who had been glad to steal a donkey's carrots only a few weeks earlier! But I did not think of that. I thought of my great talents, wasted in a provincial company. "I'll think it over," I told the agent, seeing he would not increase the amount.

"No. I must know right now," he replied firmly.

CHARLIE CHAPLIN'S OWN STORY

I wrinkled my brows with an air of indecision and thought for a minute.

"All right, I'll do it," I said.

"Rehearsal to-morrow at ten," Frank Stern said, giving me the address in a quite commonplace manner.

CHAPTER XII

In which I rehearse the part of the boy hero of the thrilling melodrama, *From Rags to Riches;* and start off on a tour of the provinces.

I saw Sidney off on the ship for Africa, having induced him to give me the cane, and as I stood waving at him I was so elated with success that I felt almost intoxicated. I was an actor at last—a real actor, with a rehearsal in prospect! I strutted up and down on the dock a bit after Sidney was gone feeling sorry for all the people about, who little realized what an important person they were passing so heedlessly. Then I took a cab again, as due to my position, and gave the driver the address of the rooms Sidney had taken for me in Burton Crescent.

I was not only an actor, but a man with an income of my own and bachelor chambers. I was very haughty with the char-woman who brought in the coals for my fire, and I sat frowning for some time in an attitude of deep thought, pondering whether I should have cream tart or apple-and-blackberry pudding

96

for dinner. At last I decided on both and ate them in state before my own fire. It was a great evening.

Next morning I was divided between my eagerness to hurry to the rehearsal and my feeling that it would more accord with my importance if I should arrive a little late. It was not until the cab began to rattle over the cobbles about Covent Garden market that a sense of strangeness began to come over me, and I realized that I had never acted before and should not quite know what to do at the rehearsal. I looked from the windows of the cab at the costers' donkeys and thought what a short time ago I had envied them, woebegone and hungry as they were.

The rehearsal was in a room over a public house in Covent Garden, and as I climbed the stairs I began to feel small and a bit uncertain. When I went in the room was full of people standing about or sitting on boxes, and they all looked at me with interest. At one end, near the rough stage, was a little table with three important-looking men standing beside it, and after a look around I walked up to them.

"I am Charles Chaplin," I said, wishing I

were taller. "I am, I believe, to play leading man in your production."

They looked me over as Mr. Stern had done, rather sharply, and then introduced themselves. The man in the dirty plaid waistcoat was Joe Baxter, manager of *From Rags to Riches,* and also the villain in the piece. The company had been playing for a ten-weeks' round of the suburbs and was now about to go into the provinces. They were already delayed by the illness of the lead, which Mr. Baxter cursed roundly, and his chief interest in me was the hope that I was a quick study. I assured him that I was, and without any further talk he began to read the play to me.

It appeared that I was to play the boy hero, an earl's son, defrauded of my rights by the villain after my mother had pitifully died in the streets of London with property snow sifted on her from the flies. I wandered in rags through three acts, which contained a couple of murders, a dozen hair-breadth escapes, and comic relief by the comedian, and I came triumphantly into my own in the fourth act, where the villain died a terrible death.

Now whether my liking for mimicry came to

my aid or whether my own experiences, so much like those of the part I was to play, had given me material which I used unconsciously, I do not know, but when Mr. Baxter gave me my part and asked me to read it, I did it well. Mr. Baxter stood chewing his cigar when I had finished, and the look on his face was less discontented.

"Orl right," he said briskly. "Now, ladies and gents, ready! First act, second scene, Lord Plympton's droring-room! You walk through this and read your part," he said to me. "No time for study, got to play Sweetbay to-morrow night. Do the best you can with it."

The woman who was to play my mother came over while I stood waiting with the part in my hand. She was a thin sallow woman in a bright red waist and a hat with blue and yellow feathers.

"Have a toffy?" she said, holding out a bag.

"No, thanks. I left off eating them years ago," I answered, swinging my cane.

"Horrid play, aren't it?" she went on. "Beastly life, on tour. How do you like your part?"

"Oh," I answered carelessly, "it's not much

99

of a part, but I do what I can with it. I won't mind the provinces for a season. I'm tired of London."

"Here you, Reginald—Chaplett, whatever your name is—come on!" Mr. Baxter yelled, and I started forward on to the stage. Mr. Baxter uttered such a sound, between a groan and a roar, that I stopped, startled.

"Good Gawd!" he moaned. "That's the window, you idiot! Come through the door! Come through the door! What do you think you are, a bloomin' bird?"

It was hard work, rehearsing on the bare stage, with no idea what the scenery was to be, and Mr. Baxter went from rage to profanity and from that to speechlessness and groans while he drove us through the parts. We worked all day and late into the night and he did not let me stop a minute, although I grew hungry and the smell of the fried fish the other actors ate while I was on the stage took my mind from the work. At last he let me go, with a groan.

"It couldn't well be worse!" he said grimly. "Now, ladies and gents, Waterloo station eleven sharp to-morrow, ready fer Sweetbay!"

I came very wearily down the flight of stairs holding the bundle of manuscript and my cane while the words of my part and all the stage directions buzzed together in my brain. I had not money enough for a cab; if we were to go to Sweetbay the next day I must walk back to my rooms. It was a cold foggy night and my steps sounded loud and echoing on the pavements as I hurried along, tired and hungry, almost ready to wish for a coster's cart that I might crawl into and rest. But I held as firmly as I could to the thought that I was an actor, though finding small comfort in it, and when at last I had reached my rooms I had persuaded myself that I was driven by the duties and ambitions of a great position. So I scowled fiercely at my reflection in the mirror over the mantel, and tying a towel about my head so as to look the character of a diligent student, I sat all night reading the words of my part and committing them to memory.

Next morning, when I reached the station with my bag, the rest of the company was waiting, very draggled and weary looking, while Mr. Baxter bustled about, swearing loudly. My spirits rose at the noise and excitement of

101

the starting, and when I saw the compartment labeled, "Reserved: *From Rags to Riches* company," I held my head proudly again, hoping that passers-by would notice and say to each other, "See! He must be the leading man."

I lingered on the platform until the last minute, looking as important as I could and thinking how well the cane carried out the effect, and then, as the engine began to puff and the train slowly started, I swung myself aboard and walked into the compartment where the company was settling itself for the trip to Sweetbay.

CHAPTER XIII

In which I encounter the difficulties of a make-up box; make my first appearance in drama; and learn the emptiness of success with no one to share it.

THE rest of the company were very glum on that journey to Sweetbay, sitting hunched up any way in their seats and looking drearily from the windows, not even glancing at me as I strode up and down the compartment, murmuring the words of my part to myself and hoping Mr. Baxter was noticing how studious I was.

"Well enough for you, old man," I said to myself, seeing him absorbed in a copy of *Floats* and not even looking in my direction. "Wait till you see me act!" But I felt my spirits somewhat dampened by his indifference, nevertheless.

When the train stopped at Sweetbay I stepped to the platform with a lively air and stood looking around while the others dragged down the steps. It was raining a little, very

103

few people were about and they were not at all interested in us, which seemed to me a personal affront.

"Hustle, now! No time to look for lodgings till after matinée!" Mr. Baxter said briefly, and set off at a brisk pace, the rest of us straggling behind him through the streets.

I walked as jauntily as possible, swinging my cane with an air, but the gloom of it all depressed me. I wished myself older than twelve years, and larger, so that I would not have to look up at the others, and I wondered if I could do the make-up right, but determined not to ask any one how it was done. I had bought a make-up box and experimented a bit before my mirror, but I was doubtful of the effect on the stage.

When we reached the Theater Royal, a dark smelly place, with littered, dirty dressing-rooms, I felt quite helpless before the problem. It appeared that all the men were to share one dressing-room, and I crowded into the tiny place with the others and opened my make-up box, ashamed of its new look. The comedian and Lord Plympton, who behind the scenes was a sallow gloomy individual with a breath smelling of beer and onions, sat down at once in their shirt-sleeves before the small cracked mirrors and began smearing their faces with grease-paint, for we were late, and already the lights had gone on in front and a few people were shuffling in.

I made shift with the make-up as best I might and hurried into the ragged suit I was to wear in the first scene, pinning it up in small folds about me, for it was the costume worn by the former lead and too large for me. However, I hoped to make it do, and when, by the glimpses I could get of myself in the mirror, it seemed to be all right, I left the dressing-room and wandered into the wings, feeling well satisfied with myself.

The stage was shadowy and dark behind the big canvas scenes. "A street in a London slums" was already set, and the scene shifters, swearing in hoarse whispers, were wheeling Lord Plympton's drawing-room into position for a quick change. I made my way warily around this and encountered Mr. Baxter, who was rushing about in a frenzy, roundly cursing everything in sight. When he saw me he stopped short.

"Good Gord!" he cried. "Going on like this?"

"What's wrong?" I asked, startled.

"Wrong? Wrong? Why was I ever a manager?" moaned Mr. Baxter, seizing his head in both hands. "You gory idiot!" he exploded, and seemed to choke.

"What's the row, Joe?" the woman who was to play my mother asked, coming over to us, while I stood very uneasy and doubtful what to say.

"Look at 'im!" roared Mr. Baxter. "How many times have I told him he's pathetic— PATHETIC! And here he comes with a face like a bloomin' cranberry! And he goes on in six minutes!"

"I'll look out for the lad," the woman said, kindly enough, and taking me by the hand she led me into the women's dressing-room, where she made up my face with her own paint and powder and I squirmed with humiliation.

"It's your first shop, aren't it?" she said, drawing the dark circles under my eyes, and I drew myself up with as much dignity as possible in the circumstances and said stiffly,

106

"This is my first engagement with a provincial company."

Then I returned to the wings and waited with beating heart for my cue. Mr. Baxter, made up as the villain now, stood beside me giving me last orders, but my head whirled so I could hardly hear him, and all the lights made a dazzling glare in my eyes. Then my cue came—my mother, on the stage, moaned piteously, and Mr. Baxter gave me a little push. I stumbled out on the stage, crying, "See, mother dear, here is a crust!"

The blinding glare in my eyes and the confusion in my brain were over in a minute. The strangeness of it all fell away from me, and, in a manner I can not explain to one who is not an actor, I was at the same time the ragged, hungry child, starving in Covent Garden market, and the self-conscious actor playing a part. I wept sincerely for the suffering of my poor mother, who moaned at my feet, and at the same time I said to myself, proudly, "What, ho! now they see how pathetic I am, what?" When I did not remember the words I made them up, paying no heed to the villain's anxious prompting behind his hand, and I defied him vigorously at the close of the act, crying, "You shall touch my mother only over my dead body!" with enthusiasm. The curtain fell and there was a burst of applause behind it.

"Not half bad, what?" I said triumphantly to Mr. Baxter, while my stage mother scrambled to her feet, and he replied moodily, "Don't be so cocky, young 'un. There's three acts yet to go."

But I was warmed up to the work now and I enjoyed it, wandering forlorn through my imitation griefs and at last coming grandly into my rights as the earl's son and wearing the splendor of the velvet suit with great aplomb in the last act, although I was obliged surreptitiously to hold up the trousers with one hand because I could not find enough pins in the dressing-room to make them fit me. I felt that I was the hit of the piece and rushed out of the theater afterward to find lodgings and eat a chop before the evening performance with all the emotions of an actor who had arrived at the pinnacle of fame. I could not forbear telling the waiter who served me the chop, a grimy little eating house not far from

108

the theater, that I was the leading man of the *From Rags to Riches* company and must be served quickly, as pressing duties awaited me at the theater before the evening performance. He looked down at me with a broad grin on his fat face and said, "You don't say, now!" in a highly gratifying tone, although I wished he had said it more solemnly.

That night, sitting alone in my bed-sitting-room in actors' lodgings, I was greatly pleased with myself and wished only that my mother were there to see me. I wrote her a long letter, telling her how well I had done and promised to send her at least ten shillings, and perhaps a pound, when I was paid on Saturday. Then I went out into the dark silent streets where the rain fell mournfully to post it. The night was very gloomy. After all, I was only twelve and had no friends anywhere except Sidney, who had gone to Africa. I thought of my mother lying alone in the hospital and perhaps not able to understand my glad news when it should arrive, and such a feeling of sadness and loneliness came over me that I hurried back to my room and crawled into bed without lighting the gas, very unhappy, indeed.

CHAPTER XIV

In which I taste the flavor of success; get unexpected
word from my mother; and face new responsibil-
ities.

HOWEVER, though I never entirely forgot my
mother in London, I enjoyed the life on tour
with the *From Rags to Riches* company, with
all the excitement of catching trains and finding different lodgings in each town, and I
never understood the grumblings of the others
when we traveled all night and had to rush
to a matinée without resting. I liked it all;
I liked the thrill of having to pause in a scene
while the audience applauded, as they did
pretty often after I became used to the stage.
I liked standing with the others after the Saturday matinées, when Mr. Baxter came around
giving each one his salary, and I had great
fun afterward jingling the two pounds in my
pocket and feeling very wealthy and important
when I spent sixpence for a copy of *Floats*.

110

Best of all I like lying late in bed Sunday mornings, as I could do sometimes, and looking for my name in the provincial journals— "Charles Chaplin, as Reginald, showed an artistic appreciation which gives promise of a brilliant future," or "Charles Chaplin, the talented young actor, plays the part of Reginald with feeling."

Then, though no one could see me, I would pretend great indifference, yawning wearily and saying: "Oh, very well for a provincial journal, but wait till we get to London!" But I always saved the clippings.

I became friendly with the comedian, who was a fat good-humored fellow enough, and always got a laugh in the third act by sitting on an egg. I sometimes treated him to oysters after the show on Saturday nights, and he used to grumble about the stage, saying: "It's a rotten life, lad, a rotten life. You'd be well out of it." Then he would shake his head mournfully and stop a great sigh by popping an oyster into his mouth.

"It suits me, old top," I would reply, with a wave of my hand, thinking that when I was his age I would have London at my feet.

111

I did not care much for the others in the company, as I felt they greatly underrated my importance, and I especially shunned Cora, the woman who played my mother, because she was inclined to make a small boy of me behind the scenes, and would inquire if my socks were darned or if my underwear were warm, no matter who was present.

In the spring the tour of *From Rags to Riches* came to an end. For the last time I clutched my stage mother while the paper snow was sifted on us from the flies; for the last time I defied the villain and escaped the murderer and wore the velvet suit, very shabby now, but fitting better, when I came back to Lord Plympton's drawing-room.

I felt very depressed and lonely when I came off the stage. The company was breaking up, most of them were gone already, and the "Street in a London Slum" had been loaded into a wagon with "The Thieves' Den" and "The Thames at Midnight." No one was in sight but the grubby scene shifters, who were swearing while they struggled with Lord Plympton's drawing-room, and the dressing-room was deserted by all but the comedian,

112

who was very drunk, and said mournfully: "It's a rotten life, it's a rotten life."

I dressed quickly and went back to my lodgings, wondering with a sinking heart what I should do next. I had seen enough of stage life by that time to realize that it was not easy to get a hearing on the Strand, and for the first time I took small comfort in the thought of my pile of clippings from the provincial journals. My rooms were cold and dark, but no gloomier than my mood when I went in, hunting in my pockets for a match to light the gas.

When the gas flared up I saw a letter propped against the cold pasty set out for my supper. I took it up, surprised, for it was the first letter I had ever received, and then I saw on the envelope the name of the parish hospital where I had left my mother.

I tore it open quickly, but my hands were shaking so it seemed a long time before I could get the sheet of paper out of the envelope. I held it close to the gas and read it. It said that my mother had asked them to write and say she was glad I was doing so well. She was able to leave the hospital now if I could take her away, or should they send her to the almshouse, as she was not strong enough to work?

I could not eat or sleep that night. Some time about dawn the landlady came knocking at my door and spoke bitterly through the panels about my wasting her gas, threatening to charge it extra on the bill. I said I was packing, paid her for the lodging, and told her to go away. Then I went out with my bags, in a very dark and chilly morning, when the early carts were beginning to rattle through the empty streets. I rode up to London on the first train, my mind torn between joy and a sort of panic, confused with a dozen plans, all of which seemed valueless.

My mother was sitting up in bed with Sidney's shawl wrapped about her when I was allowed to see her. Her hair was longer and curled about her face, but there were dark circles under her eyes and she looked very little, almost like a child.

"My, my, what a great lad you've grown!" she said, and then she began to cry. The least excitement made her sob, and her hands trembled all the while I was there.

"Never you mind, mother; I'll take care of
you!" I said briskly, and I told her what a
great success I had become on the stage. It
was the first pose I had ever taken which did
not deceive myself, for I wondered, miserably,
while I talked, what we should do if I could
get no engagement. I promised to take her
soon to beautiful lodgings, and the words
sounded hollow to me as I said them, but she
seemed pleased and was greatly cheered when
I left her. Without stopping to look for lodgings for myself, I hurried at once to the Strand,
eager to see the agents.

Now in the success or failure of an actor a
great deal depends on luck, as I was very willing to admit later when it turned against me,
although in the early days I ascribed all my
good fortune to my own great merit. On that
day when I walked down the Strand I passed
dozens of actors who had been struggling for
years to find a foothold on the stage, going
from one small part to another, with months
of starvation between, furbishing up their
shabby clothes and walking endless miles up
and down the stairs to the agents' offices in
vain. The numbers of them appalled me.

Frank Stern's outer office was full of them and they did not leave off watching his door with hungry eyes to look at me when I walked in and gave my card to the office boy.

"Can't see you," he said briefly, without looking at it. "No use the rest of you waiting, either," he said raising his voice. "He won't see nobody else to-day."

They rose and began to straggle out, some of them protesting with the office boy, who only looked at them contemptuously, repeating, "He won't see nobody." I was following them when Frank Stern's door opened and he appeared.

"Oh, hello, my lad!" he said genially. "You're just the chap I want to see. Come in, come in!" He ushered me into his inner office, clapping me on the shoulder.

CHAPTER XV

In which I understand why other people fall; burn
my bridges behind me; and receive a momentous
telegram.

THIS time I sat in Frank Stern's office with
no inflated opinion of my own importance, only
hoping, with a fast-beating heart, that he
would offer me some place with a salary. I
could hardly hear what he said for thinking of
the few coins in my pocket and my mother in
the hospital waiting for me to come back and
take her to the beautiful lodgings I had promised to engage.

"Joe Baxter tells me you did fairly well on
tour," the agent said, after an idle remark or
two. "He's taking out *Jim, the Romance of
a Cockney* in a few weeks. How would you
like the lead?"

"I'd like it," I said eagerly, and realized the
next minute I had done myself out of a raise
in the pay by not asking first how much it
would be. But the relief of having a part was
so great that I did not much care.

117

I came whistling down the stairs after I had left Frank Stern, and in the Strand I looked with a different eye on the actors I passed, beginning to think that, after all, they must lack real merit such as I had, or else they drank or were not willing to work. I saw the comedian from the *From Rags to Riches* company, looking very seedy, and was passing him with a nod when he stopped me.

"How's tricks?" he asked of me. "Shopped yet?"

"Oh, yes, I have an engagement," I replied carelessly, swinging my cane. "Only a provincial company, but not so bad."

"I say, not really?" he said, surprised. "You're in luck. Look here, old chap, could you lend me five bob?"

"Well, no," I answered. "No, I'm afraid not. But I hope you're shopped soon. You ought to quit drinking, you know—you'd do better."

"Well enough for you to talk, my lad. You'll think different when you've been tramping the Strand for twenty years, like I have, and never a decent chance in the whole of them. You're on top now, but you'll find

it's not all beer and skittles before you've done.
I say, make it three bob—or two?"

I gave him a shilling and he begged me to
say a word to Baxter for him, which I meant
to do, but later forgot. Then I went search-
ing lodgings for my mother. I found them
in a private home for convalescents in Burton
Crescent—very decent rooms with a little bal-
cony overlooking a small park, and Mrs.
Dobbs, the landlady, seemed a pleasant person
and promised to look out for my mother while
I was on tour.

My mother was delighted when she saw the
place, laughing and crying at the same time,
while I wrapped her in Sidney's shawl and
made her comfortable with some cushions on
the couch before the fire. We had tea together
very cozily, and I told her I should soon be
a great London actor, which she firmly believed, only saying I was too modest and made
a mistake in going on tour when I should have
at least a good part in a West End theater.

By closest economy I managed to send her
a pound every week during that season with
Jim, the Romance of a Cockney, though sometimes going without supper to buy the en-

velope and stamp; and because it is not poverty, but economy, which teaches the value of a penny, I learned it so thoroughly that year that I have never forgotten it. The only part of the tour which I enjoyed was the time I spent on the stage, when I forgot my constant thought of money and lived the romantic joys and griefs of Jim. I played the part so well, perhaps for this reason, that I was becoming known as one of the most promising boy actors in England, and I used to clip every mention of my acting which I could find and send it to my mother in the Saturday letter.

When I came back to London at the close of the season I expected nothing less than a rush of the managers to engage me. I walked into Frank Stern's office very chesty and important with not even a glance for the office boy or the crowd of actors patiently waiting and knocked on his door with my cane. Then I pushed it open and went in.

Frank Stern was sitting with his feet on his desk, smoking and reading *Floats* in great contentment. He leaped to his feet when he heard me walk in, but when he saw who it was he welcomed me boisterously.

120

"Glad to see you back, glad to see you!" he said jovially. "Sit down."

"No, thanks. I just dropped in to see what you had to offer for next season," I said carelessly. "It must be something good this time, you know."

His cordiality dropped like a mask; he looked at me very sternly.

"There's a part in *His Mother Left Him to Starve*," he said. "We could use you in that."

"How much salary?" I asked.

"Two pounds," he answered sharply.

"No, thanks," I said airily. "Though I won't say I mightn't consider it for four."

"Then I'm afraid I haven't anything," he said, and turned back to his desk as though he were very busy. I went out whistling, so sure of my value that I was careless of offending him. And indeed when, ten days later, I was offered the part of Billy, the page, in *Sherlock Holmes*, at a salary of thirty shillings, I was sure that I had acted astutely, and gave myself credit for good business sense as well as great talent. I even had some thoughts of holding out for a part in the Lon-

121

don company, and if I had had a few shillings more, or any money to pay for my mother's lodgings, I might have been foolish enough to do it.

As it was, I walked into the rooms where the company was rehearsing with a feeling that it was a condescension on my part to go on tour again, and marching briskly up to the prompter's table, laid my cane upon it—a breach of theatrical etiquette at which the company stood aghast. I never did it again, for that day's work with a real stage manager gave me my first idea of good acting, and I left late that night with my vanity smarting painfully.

"'Act natural!'" I said to myself, bitterly mocking the stage manager. "'Talk like a human being!' My eye, what do they think the people want? I act like an actor, I talk like an actor, and if they don't like it they can jolly well take their old show! I can get better!"

Nevertheless, I went back next day and worked furiously under the scathing sarcasm and angry oaths of the manager until I had learned the part passably well and forgotten most of the stage tricks I had found so effective in *From Rags to Riches*. The night before we went on tour I had dinner with my mother, who was still in the care of Mrs. Hobbs, so thin and nervous that it worried me to see her, and she was fluttering with excitement and overjoyed at my being a great actor, but for the first time I doubted it.

However, the press notices speedily brought back my self-confidence. In almost every town they praised my work so highly that the actor who played Holmes gave me cold glances whenever he saw me and even cut bits of my part. Then, though complaining bitterly, I knew I had really "arrived," and I openly grinned at him before the company, and demanded a better dressing-room.

Just before the close of the tour I was standing in the wings one evening confiding to one of the actresses my intention of placing a bent pin in Holmes' chair on the stage next evening, where I calculated it would have great effect, owing to his drawing his dressing gown tight around him with a dignified air just before sitting down, when a boy came up and gave me a telegram. I tore it open, fearing bad news from my mother, and read it. It said:

"William Gillette opens in *Sherlock Holmes* here next week. Wants you for Billy. Charles Frohman."

William Gillette!   Charles Frohman!

CHAPTER XVI

In which I journey to London; meet and speak with
a wax-works figure; and make my first appearance
in a great theater.

I DO not know how I got through my act that
night. I was in such a flurry of excitement and
so jubilant over the great news that I missed
my cues and played with only half my wits
on my work, careless how Holmes frowned
at me. Every one in the company had heard
of my telegram from Frohman before the end
of the second act, and I knew they were watching me enviously from the wings. I rushed
past them, in wild haste to get to the dressing-
room and take off my make-up as soon as my
last scene was finished, and I was half dressed
while they were taking the curtain call.

I met Holmes and the manager just outside
the dressing-room and resigned my place in
their company with great haughtiness.

"Of course—er—you understand that I—
er—can not do justice to my art as long as
I am supported by merely provincial actors,"

I said, looking at Holmes as majestically as I might from a height two feet less than his. Then I drew the manager aside and said kindly, "Of course, old man, I appreciate all you've done, and all that—any time I can do anything for you with Frohman, you understand, you've only to say the word."

The entire company, excepting only Holmes, was at the station to see me off next morning, and since in the meantime my first vainglory had diminished and I felt more my usual self, there was a jolly half-hour before the train left. Every one wished me luck and promised to come to see me act in London, while I assured them I would not forget old friends, and the manager clapped me heartily on the back and said he'd always known I would do great things. They gave a great cheer when the train started and I waved at them from the back platform. Then I was off, to London and fame.

Early the next afternoon, dressed in a new suit with new shirt and tie to match, I arrived at the Duke of York's Theater in the West End and inquired for the stage manager. I had to wait for him a minute on the dim stage

126

and I stood looking out over the rows of empty seats in the big dark house, thrilling to think that before long they would be filled with scores of persons watching me act. Then Mr. Postham came hurrying up, a very busy man with a quick nervous voice. I told him who I was, and he gave me the manuscript of my part in a hurried manner.

"That's all. Rehearsal here, nine to-morrow," he said. Then, as I was turning away, he added, "Like to see Mr. Gillette?"

"I would, yes," I answered eagerly, and tried to clutch at my self-possession, which I had never lacked before, while the boy led me through the dim passages to Mr. Gillette's dressing-room. The boy knocked at the door of it, said loudly, "Mr. Chaplin to see Mr. Gillette," and left me standing there, breathing hard.

An instant later the door opened and a little Japanese, perfectly dressed in the clothes of an English man-servant, popped into the aperture. I had never seen a Japanese servant before, and his appearance so confounded me that I could only look at him and repeat what the boy had said, while I fumbled in my pocket for a card and wondered if it would be proper to give it to him if I should find one. It appeared that it was not necessary, for he opened the door wider. I stepped in.

William Gillette was sitting before his dressing-table, busy with make-up. He rose to meet me—a very tall stately man, his face entirely covered with dead white paint. The whole place was white—the walls, the dressing-table, even the floor, as I remember it—and the whiteness was intensified by a glare of strong white light. In that bright glare, and under the mask of white paint, Mr. Gillette did not seem like a real man. He seemed like some fantastic curio in a glass case.

"You're to play Billy, I understand," he said, looking keenly at me through narrow, almost almond, eyes. "How old are you?"

"Fourteen, sir," I answered as if hypnotized, for I was now telling every one that I was sixteen.

"I hear you're a very promising young actor," he said. "I hope you'll make a good Billy—what did you want to see me about?"

"I just wanted to see you," I replied.

"Well, I'm very glad we've met," he said,

looking amused, I thought. "If I can be any help to you, come again, won't you?"

I think I replied suitably as I backed out. I reached the street before I quite recovered from the effect of his strange appearance in that white room. I had met one of the greatest actors on the English stage, and I felt as though I had seen a figure in a wax-works and it had spoken to me.

Then, when I stood on the curb in all the noise of the London traffic, I realized that the events of that momentous day were all real. I was engaged to play with William Gillette in the finest of West End theaters; I held the manuscript of my part in my hand. Excited and jubilant, I rushed off to tell my mother the great news, and then to engage lodgings of my own, where I spent all that evening walking up and down, rehearsing the part of Billy, only pausing now and then, with a whoop, to do a few dance steps or stand on my head.

The next morning I was one of the first to reach the theater for rehearsal. I had risen early to take a few turns up and down the Strand, hoping to meet some one I knew to whom I could mention casually that I was with Frohman now, but every one I passed was a stranger and I had to content myself with looking haughtily at them and saying to myself: *"You* wouldn't half like to be on your way to rehearsal with William Gillette, would you now? What, ho!"

Mr. Postham proved to be different from the stage managers I had known before. He was nervous and excitable, but no matter how badly an actor read his lines, Mr. Postham never swore at him.

"No," he said quietly. *"This* way, 'I'll do it, sir.' No, not 'I'll do *it,* sir,' but 'I'll *do* it, sir.' Try it again. No, that's a little too emphatic. Listen, 'I'll do it, sir.' Not quite so self-confident. Again, 'I'll do it, sir.' Once more, please." He never seemed to grow tired. He kept us at it for hours, watching every detail, every inflection or shade of tone, and his patience was endless. It was new work to me, but I liked it; and after rehearsal I would practise for hours in my rooms, liking the sound of my voice in the different tones.

William Gillette had come to London with a play called *Clarice,* which had not gone well.

130

William Gillette as *Sherlock Holmes*

He was putting on *Sherlock Holmes* to save the season and rushing rehearsals in order to have the new play ready in the shortest possible time. We worked all day, and twice were called for midnight rehearsals, after *Clarice* was off the boards. Two weeks after I reached London we were called at seven in the morning for dress rehearsal. *Sherlock Holmes* was to be put on that night.

Everything went wrong at the dress rehearsal. We were overworked and nervous; we missed our cues; some of the properties were lost; Mr. Postham was intensely quiet. I was very well pleased by it all, for every East End actor knows that a bad dress rehearsal means a good first performance, but the manager and Mr. Gillette did not seem to share my opinion, and the company scattered gloomily enough when at last they let us go, with admonitions to be early at the theater that night.

I was made up and dressed for the first scene early, and hurried out to the peep-hole in the curtain, hoping to catch a glimpse of my mother in the audience. I had got tickets for her and Mrs. Hobbs and ordered a carriage

131

for them, as my mother was not strong and could not come in a tram. The house was filling fast. Behind the scenes there was tense breathless excitement; scene shifters and stage carpenters were hurrying back and forth; there was a furious scene over something mislaid. Every one's nerves were strained to the breaking point.

The curtain went up. From the wings, where I stood waiting for my cue and saying my lines over and over to myself with a tight feeling in my throat, I saw Mr. Gillette opening the scene. I listened carefully to every word he spoke, knowing that every one brought my entrance nearer. Suddenly Mr. Postham touched my shoulder.

"Royalty's in front," he said. "Whatever you do, don't look at the royal box."

Then, on the stage, Mr. Gillette spoke my cue. I put back my shoulders, cleared my throat, and stepped out on the stage, my brain repeating, "Don't look at the royal box."

CHAPTER XVII

In which I play with a celebrated actor; dare to look at the royal box; pay a penalty for my awful crime; gain favor with the public; and receive a summons from another famous star.

My nerves were stretched tight, like badly tuned violin strings, and I seemed to feel them vibrate when I stepped on the stage and spoke my opening line, with Gillette's eyes upon me and the packed house listening. My brain was keyed to a high pitch, working smoothly, but it did not seem in any way attached to my body, and I heard the words as though some one else had spoken them. They were clear, firm, the accent perfect. I felt myself stepping three steps forward, one to the right, and turning to Mr. Gillette; heard my second line spoken, with the emphasis placed properly on the third word.

"Don't look at the royal box," I said to myself.

Then I was in the swing of the scene. Mr. Gillette spoke; I answered him; the situation came clearly into my mind. I realized that

133

I was playing opposite William Gillette, that the eyes of London were on me, and royalty itself listening. I threw myself into the work, quivering with the strain of it, but determined to play up to the big moment. I was doing well. I knew it. I saw it in the relaxation of Mr. Gillette's anxious watching. He was abandoning himself to his part, trusting me to play up to him.

"Now, Billy, listen to me carefully," he said. I turned my head to the right angle, felt the muscles of my face quiver with the exact expression that should be there.

"Yes, sir," I replied, with the exact tone of eagerness I had practised so often. Gillette took up his lines. The scene was going well. The house hung breathless on every word.

"Don't look at the royal box," I repeated to myself, feeling an almost irresistible longing to turn my head in that direction, and stiffening my neck against it.

I did not know who was in the box and would have been no wiser if I had looked, for I had never seen the royal family, but I learned later. The late King Edward himself was present, with Queen Alexandria, the King of

Greece, Prince Christian and the Duke of Connaught. Prince Christian, who was a personal friend of William Gillette, came often to see him act, but this was an unusually brilliant party.

I stood tense, waiting for my cue. It came at last.

"Billy, I want you to watch the thieves," said Sherlock Holmes.

It was a thrilling moment in the play. I must be silent just long enough—not too long —before I spoke. I heard my heart beat in the pause; the audience waited, tense. The house was silent.

Then, in the stillness, we heard a murmur from Prince Christian, and an impatient stage whisper in reply from the King of Greece.

"Don't tell me—don't tell me; I want to see it," he said. "Jove, watch that youngster!"

The tension of my nerves broke. William Gillette, in an effort to save the dramatic moment of the scene, repeated, "Billy, I want you to watch the thieves." And, while the house gazed at me, I turned my head and looked full at the royal box.

The audience was stunned. It sat dumb, in

frozen horror. There was an awful silence, while I stood helpless, gazing at the King of Greece, and he stared back at me with slowly widening eyes. Then his face broke into little lines; they ran down from his eyes to his mouth; it widened into a smile. A sudden chuckle from King Edward broke the terrible stillness. Again we heard the voice of the King of Greece:

"By Jove! Ha! Ha!"

I tore my eyes away and continued the scene through a haze. We finished it before a silent house. The curtain fell. Then, led by the royal box, a storm of applause arose. We took our curtain call—I was on the stage of a great West End theater, bowing before applauding crowds, in the company of one of the greatest actors in London. The voice of royalty itself had been heard speaking of my acting. I was dizzy with exultation.

The curtain fell for the last time and I strutted proudly from the stage, looking from one to another of the company, eager to meet their envious looks. They hurried to their dressing-rooms without a glance at me. No one spoke. There was a strained chill feeling

136

in the atmosphere. I passed Mr. Postham and he hurried by me as if I were not there.

A feeling of trouble and loneliness grew upon me while I touched up my make-up for the second scene, though I told myself as confidently as possible that my looking at the royal box could not have been so bad, since the King of Greece had smiled and Mr. Postham had said nothing. Yet I would have been more at ease if he had sworn at me.

I threw myself into the work of the remaining scenes with all the skill I had learned, and I felt that I was doing them well, but the cold feeling of uncertainty and doubt grew upon me. At last the final curtain fell. Then for the first time that evening the eyes of the whole company turned on me. They lingered on the stage, waiting. Mr. Postham walked slowly out and looked at me quietly.

"Well, it went well, didn't it?" I said cockily to him, saying savagely to myself that I had been the hit of the evening. My words fell on a dead silence, while Mr. Postham continued to look at me, and little by little I felt myself growing very small and would have liked to go away, but could not.

"I suppose you realize what you did," Mr. Postham said, after a long time, and paused. I opened my mouth, but could not say a word.

"It is fortunate—very fortunate—that His Majesty—was pleased—to overlook it," Mr. Postham continued slowly. He paused again. "Fined three pounds," he said briskly, then, and walked away. So I went meekly from the scene of my first appearance in a good theater under the scornful and surprised glances of the other actors, who had expected to see the part taken from me, and I said bitterly to myself that if *this* was the reward of talent on the stage—!

I did good work that season with William Gillette, as all the press notices showed. Every morning, lying luxuriously in bed in my lodgings, I pored over the London journals, seizing eagerly on every comment on my acting, reading and rereading it. I was the "most promising young actor on the English stage," I was "doing clever work," I was "the best Billy London has seen yet." To me, as I gazed at these notices, William Gillette was merely "also mentioned." I felt that I alone was making the play a success and I walked afterward up and down the Strand in a glow of pride and self-confidence, dressed in all the splendor money could buy, swinging my cane, nodding carelessly to the men I knew and picturing them saying to each other after I had passed, "He is the great actor at the Duke of York's Theater. I knew him once."

The season was drawing to a close and, learning that William Gillette was returning to America, I confidently expected nothing less than an invitation to return with him, when one day I arrived at the theater early and found a note awaiting me. I tore it open carelessly and read:

"Will you please call at St. James' Theater to-morrow afternoon? I should like to see you.
                                    "Mrs. Kendall."

"Oh, ho! Mrs. Kendall!" I said to myself. "Well, she will have to offer something good to get *me!*"

CHAPTER XVIII

In which I refuse an offer to play in the provinces;
make my final appearance as Billy at the Duke
of York's Theater; and suffer a bitter disappointment.

I ASSUMED a slightly bored air while I glanced
through the note again. Oh, yes, Mrs. Kendall! The greatest actress in London. Well,
I would call on her if she liked; I would just
drop in and see what she had to offer. Something good, no doubt, but I should soon show
her that it would have to be something very
good indeed if she hoped to get *me*.

I flipped the note under the dressing-table
and began to make up, wondering what America would prove to be like, picturing to myself
the enthusiasm of American reporters when it
was known that William Gillette was bringing
England's greatest boy actor to New York
with him.

"Curtain!" cried the call boy down the corridors. I called him in, hastily scribbled off a
note to Mrs. Kendall, saying that I would call
at twelve next day, and gave it to the call boy

140

to post. Then I went out, nodding affably to the other actors, and took my place in the wings to await my cue.

"Too bad the season's closing, isn't it?" said Irene Vanbrugh, who stood beside me.

"Oh, it's been a pleasant season enough, as seasons go," I replied carelessly. "The deuce of it is, there's no rest between 'em when one has made a hit. Rehearsals and all that."

"Y-yes," she said, looking at me queerly.

"And it's such a bore, so many people after one," I continued. "Now, there's Mrs. Kendall, very pleasant woman and all that—had another note from her just now. Suppose I'll have to run around and see her again."

"Oh, I say, Mrs. Kendall—not really!" Miss Vanbrugh cried, in such a tone of awe that it annoyed me. Mrs. Kendall was well enough, I said to myself, but I was the greatest boy actor in England. I took my cue confidently, glad not to be bothered with any more of Miss Vanbrugh's conversation.

The next day at noon I arrived at Mrs. Kendall's hotel, humming a bit and swinging a new cane, very well pleased with myself, for the notices in the London journals had been very good indeed that day. I noticed that the lift boy recognized me and seemed properly impressed, and I stepped into Mrs. Kendall's sitting-room disposed to be quite affable to her.

She was not there. I waited five minutes and still she had not come. I began to be irritated. What, keeping me waiting! I glanced at my watch, walked up and down a minute, very much bored with such lack of consideration on her part. Then I determined to leave and show her I was not to be trifled with in such a manner. Just as I took up my cane the door opened and Mrs. Kendall entered. She was a pleasant matronly-looking woman with tired lines around her eyes and a quiet gentle manner.

"I'm afraid I have just a minute," I said, ostentatiously looking at my watch again.

"I'm very sorry to have kept you waiting," she answered in a soft low voice. "We understand your season with Mr. Frohman is ending next week. Mr. Kendall and I have seen your work. We are taking out a company for a forty-weeks' tour in the provinces, and there is a part with us which we think you would fill very well."

I looked at her with raised eyebrows.

"In the provinces?" I said coldly. "I am very sorry, madam, but I could not think of leaving London." I took up my cane again and rose briskly.

Mrs. Kendall looked at me a moment with a tired smile about her lips. Then she rose, said that in that case she regretted having taken up my time, and told me good-by very pleasantly.

"She sees she can not offer *me* anything!" I said proudly to myself, putting back my shoulders importantly as I came down in the lift. I walked through the hotel lounging-room with a quick brisk step, called a cab and said to the driver in a loud voice, so the by-standers might guess who I was, "Duke of York's Theater, and be quick about it, my man!"

I awaited confidently an offer from Froh-man to bring me to New York with William Gillette, determining when it came to insist on an increase in salary. Every evening I ex-pected to find a note from him in my dressing-room, and I met the gloomy glances of the other actors with a wise smile and a knowing

143

look. They might be troubled with the prospect of an uncertain future, I said to myself, but I was secure. I had made the hit of the piece, as the nightly applause showed.

The last week of *Sherlock Holmes* drew to a close, and with a sinking heart I realized that no offer had come from Frohman. I played my part every night with all the skill I knew, and hearing the house echo and echo again with loud applause, I said to myself, "*Now* Frohman will see how badly he needs me!" But still there was no word from him.

The last night came, and behind the scenes there was such a deep gloom that one could almost feel it like a fog. There was no joking in the dressing-rooms, the actors moodily made up and walked about the corridors afterward with strained anxious faces or laughed in a manner more gloomy than silence. The company was breaking up, no one knew what part he might find next, and all faced the prospect of wearily walking the Strand again, struggling to get a hearing with the agents, hoping against hope for a chance, growing shabbier and hungrier as they waited and hoped and saw the weeks going by.

144

For the last time I played Billy; for the last time I met Mr. Gillette's kindly glance and felt him pat my shoulder, saying, "Well done, Billy!" while the audience applauded. We stood together on the stage, bowing and smiling, while the curtain rose and fell and rose again and applause came over the footlights in crashing waves. Then the curtain fell for the last time.

"It's over," said Mr. Gillette, his shoulders drooping with weariness. Then he spoke a word or two of farewell to each of us and went to his dressing-room. The actors hurriedly took off their make-up and scattered, calling to one another in the corridor. "Well, so long, old man!" "See you later, Mabel, tata!" "Wait a minute, I'm coming!" "Good luck old fellow!"

I dressed slowly, unable to believe that this was the last night and that there was no offer from Mr. Frohman. Mr. Gillette was still in his dressing-room. I walked up and down outside his door debating whether or not to tap on it and ask him if there had not been a mistake.

"I was the hit of the play, wasn't I?" I said

defiantly to myself, but a great wave of doubt and depression had come over me and I could not bring myself to knock on that door. Suddenly it opened and Mr. Gillette came out dressed for the street. Behind him I saw the Japanese servant carrying a bag.

"Mr. Gillette," I said boldly, though my knees were unsteady. "Aren't you taking any of the company to America with you?"

"Er—oh, it's you!" he said, startled, for he had almost stumbled against me in the gloom. "No; oh, no; I'm not taking any one with me. You were a very good Billy, Charles. I hope you get something good very soon. Good-by."

CHAPTER XIX

In which my fondest hopes are shattered by cold reality; I learn the part played by luck on the Strand; and receive an unexpected appeal for help.

I STOOD there watching Mr. Gillette's back receding down the corridor. I felt stunned, unable to realize that he was really going. I could not believe that it was all over, that he did not mean to take me to America after all. He stopped once and my heart gave a great leap and began to pound loudly, but he only spoke to some one he met and then went on. He turned a corner, the little Japanese servant turned the corner after him, carrying the bag. They were gone.

I went back into my dressing-room then and made a little bundle of my stage clothes and make-up box. The stage hands had finished clearing the stage; it was bare and dim when I crossed it and came out through the stage door for the last time. A cold gray fog was drifting down the deserted street and I wished to take a cab, but it came to me suddenly that I

147

had no part now and could not afford it. I tucked my bundle under my arm and set out on foot for my lodgings.

All the way it seemed to me that I was in a bad dream—a dream where I must walk on and on and on mechanically through an unreal world of blurred lights and swirling grayness. I climbed the stairs to my lodgings at last, still with a dull hazy feeling of unreality, lighted the gas and sat down on my bed with the bundle beside me. Then it came upon me sharply that it was all true. The season was over. I was not going to America. I had only a few pounds and no prospect of getting another part.

I unfolded the little suit I had worn as Billy and looked at it for a long time, suffering as only a sensitive boy of fifteen can when he sees all his brightest hopes come to nothing. I walked up and down, clenching my hands and wishing that I might die. It was almost dawn when I folded the little suit, put it away in the farthest corner of a closet and crawled miserably to bed.

Next morning I felt brighter. After all, I had made a big hit as Billy; there must be any number of managers in London who would be glad to get me. There were no letters for me in the mail, but I said to myself that I must give them time. I would put an advertisement in *The Strand,* mentioning that I was "resting," and they would come around all right. I wrote it out carefully, dressed my best and took it down to *The Strand* office myself so there would be no delay. Then I went to see my mother and told her lightly that I had not decided just what offer to accept. I could not trouble her, for she had not recovered her strength fully and could only lie on her couch and smile happily at me, proud of my great success.

All that month my hopes gradually faded while I went from agent to agent trying to get a part. At first my name got me an interview with the agent immediately, but each one I saw told me quite courteously, quite briskly, that he had nothing whatever to offer me and I came out of each office with a sinking heart, holding my haughty pose with difficulty.

I got up early every morning to see as many agents as possible during the day, and although before the other actors I still kept my pose of being a great success, merely dropping in to pass the time of day with the agent, I felt panic growing within me. My small stock of money was gone. I pawned my watch, my clothes, at last even my bag, and hoarded the pennies desperately, dining in small, dirty eating houses on two-pence worth of stew.

I still bravely made a show of importance and success when I met the other actors tramping the Strand, lying miserably to them as they lied to me while we spent hours in the outer offices of the agents, bullied by the office boy, waiting hopelessly for a chance to see the agents. The season was far advanced and chances for a part grew smaller daily, but it was incredible to me that I should not find something—I who had made such a hit with William Gillette! Every morning I started out saying to myself that surely I should get something that day, and every night I crawled wearily into my lodgings, tired and discouraged, avoiding the landlady.

One day I determined to stand it no longer. I carefully trimmed my frayed collar and cuffs, brushed my suit and hat and went to the offices of the biggest agent of all, Mr. Braithewaite. He was a courteous gentleman and had always welcomed me politely. I walked in with my most important air.

"Mr. Braithewaite, I must have a part," I said briskly. "You know my work. You know I made a big hit with William Gillette. Now, I'll take anything you can give me, I don't care how small it is or what it pays. Haven't you something in a provincial company—even a walking-on part?"

He thought it over for some time in silence, while I heard my heart beating. Then he said slowly, "Well, there is a part—I will see. You come in to-morrow."

I came out whistling merrily, stepping high with a dizzy feeling that the pavement was unsteady under my feet. I was sure by his manner that he meant to have a part for me and all my self-complacency was restored. I flipped my cane as I passed the doors of the other agents, saying to myself, "Oh, ho! You'll see what you have missed!" and thinking that I would carelessly drop in and tell those who had treated me worst how well I was doing as soon as I should have the part. That night I spent one of my last two shillings for dinner, feasting on tripe and onions and ale in great spirits.

Next day, nervous with hope, I hurried to Mr. Braithewaite's offices and walked in confidently, so wrapped in my own thoughts that I did not notice that no actors were waiting as usual. I said briskly to the office boy, trying to keep my voice natural and steady, "Tell Mr. Braithewaite I am here. I have an appointment."

He looked at me with a long shrill whistle of surprise. Then, with great enjoyment in telling startling news, he said, "Don't tell me you 'aven't 'eard! 'E was shot by burglars last night. 'E's 'anging between life and death right now."

I remember I stumbled on the stairs once or twice, feeling numb all over and not able to walk steady. The bright sunlight outside seemed to jeer at me. My last hope was gone. I could not muster courage to start again on the endless tramp up and down the Strand or to face the other actors. I went back to my lodgings. The landlady met me on the stairs and looked steadily at me with tight lips and an eye which said, "I know you have only a shilling; what are you going to do about the rent?" I went hurriedly past her and climbed up to my room bitterly humiliated.

There was a letter waiting for me on the mantel. I seized it and tore it open, wild thoughts that at last I had an offer whirling in my brain. It was dated Paris. I looked at the signature—Sidney! Good old Sidney, I said to myself; he will help me. Then I read the letter.

"Dear Charlie," it said. "Your press notices are received and no one is gladder than I am. You know we always knew you would be a great success. How does it feel to have all London applauding? I wager you enjoy cutting a dash on the Strand, what? Well, Charlie, I am in the profession now, and not so great a success as you yet, but I have a prospect of a part in a couple of weeks perhaps. You know how it goes. Can you lend me five pounds, or even three, till I get a part? Love to mother and congratulations again to the clever one of the family.

"Your brother, Sidney."

CHAPTER XX

In which I try to drown my troubles in liquor and find them worse than before; try to make a living by hard work and meet small success; and find myself at last in a hospital bed, saying a surprising thing.

I stared stupidly at Sidney's letter for a minute and then I reread it slowly. It seemed like a horrible mockery—"cutting a dash on the Strand"—"The clever one of the family." And he wanted to borrow five pounds—or three—when I had only a shilling in the world.

It was the most bitter humiliation of my life. I who had always been so sure of my talent, who had patronized Sidney and promised so grandly to help him if he ever needed it and sent him the press notices of my great success with a condescending little note saying that it made no difference to me, I remembered him as fondly as ever—I could not send him a penny, or even buy food for myself.

After a while I took out a sheet of paper and

154

tried to write to him, but I could not manage it. I made several beginnings and chewed my pen a long time, while my shame and misery grew until I could bear it no longer. I put on my hat and went out.

Then, having made so many mistakes already and lost so much by them that I could not endure my own thoughts, I tried to make matters better by making them worse. A little way down the street was a barroom. Its windows were brightly lighted, casting a warm shining glow out into the foggy twilight, and I could hear men laughing inside. I went in, threw my shilling on the bar and called for whisky. It was strong raw stuff and made my throat burn, but standing there by the bar I felt a little self-esteem come back and said to myself that I was not beaten yet. I pushed the change back to the bartender and asked for another glass of the same.

I remember telling some one loudly who I was and declaring that I was the greatest actor in London. Somebody paid for more drinks and I drank again and told very witty stories and became amazingly clever and successful, laughing loudly and boasting of my dancing.

I did dance, and there was great applause, and more drinks and a great deal of noise, and I became fast friends with some one whom I promised to give a fine part in my next play and we drank again. In a word, I got gloriously drunk.

I woke up some time the next day in an alley, feeling very ill and more discouraged and depressed than before. When I slowly realized what had happened and that I had not a cent in the world, nor anything else but the rumpled, dirty clothes I wore, I sat with my head in my hands and groaned and loathed the thought of living. I did not want ever to stir again, but after a while I got up dizzily and managed to come out into the street. I knew I must do something.

I was in the North End of London. The dingy warehouses and dirty cobbled streets, through which the heavy vans rumbled, drawn by big, clumsy-footed horses, reminded me of the days in Covent Garden market, and I thought of the way I had lived there and wondered if I could find something to do there now. The thought of the Strand, where I had walked so many weeks, was hideous to me. I hated it.

I said to myself then that I would never be an actor again.

I found a watering trough and washed in it, splashing the cold water over my head until I felt refreshed. I determined not to go back to my lodgings, the few things I had left there would settle the small score and I did not want to face the landlady. The thought of my mother was more than I could face, too, but I said to myself that Mrs. Dobbs would keep her until I could get some work and send her the rent. Then I set out to hunt for a job.

I found one that afternoon. It was hard work, rolling heavy casks from one end of a warehouse to the other and helping to load them on vans. I was about fifteen at the time and slight, but some way I managed to do the work, though aching in every muscle long before the day was over. I got ten shillings a week and permission to sleep in the vans in the court behind the warehouse. I held the place almost a week before the foreman lost patience with me and found some one else to take my place.

I had made friends with several of the men, and one of them got me a place as driver for a milk company. This was easier work, though I had to be at it soon after midnight, driving through the cold dark morning, the horses almost pulling my arms from the sockets with every toss of their heavy heads, and delivering the milk in dark area-ways, where I stumbled sleepily on the steps. I had money enough now to pay for lodging in a dirty room without a window in a cheap lodging house, and I breakfasted and lunched on buns and stolen milk. I could not bring myself to visit my mother, but I sent her a few shillings in a letter and wrote that I was well and busy, so that she need not worry.

Then one morning the loss of the stolen milk was discovered. I had been unusually hungry and drunk too much of it. The boss swore at me furiously, and again I was out of a job. I was wandering up the street wondering what I could do next when I saw a great crowd about the door of a glass factory. It was still early, about four o'clock in the morning, but hundreds of men and boys were massed there waiting. I pushed my way into the crowd and asked what had happened.

Most of the boys locked at me sullenly and

158

would not answer, but one of them showed me
an advertisement. It read: "Boy wanted to
work in glass factory. Seven shillings a week."
My heart gave a leap, I might be the lucky one!
I pushed as close to the door as I could and
waited. At seven o'clock the door opened and
the crowd began to sway in excitement, each
one crying out eager words to the man in the
doorway.

I climbed nimbly up the back of the man before me, and gripping his neck with my knees,
called vigorously, "Here I am, sir!" My
theatrical training had taught me how to use
my voice, the man heard me above the uproar
and looked at me.

"I want an experienced boy in the cooling
room," he said. "Had any experience?"

"Oh, yes, sir!" I answered, while the man on
whose back I crouched tried to pull me down.

"All right, come in and I'll try you," the
man in the doorway answered, and while the
others fell back, disappointed, I crushed
through the crowd and rushed in.

The work proved to be carrying bottles from
the furnace room to the cooling place. I went
at it with a will, hurrying from the terrifically

heated room into the cold air with the heavy trays and back again as fast as I could. No matter how fast I ran there were always more bottles waiting than I could get out in time and the half-naked men, sweltering in the furnace heat, swore at me while I jumped back and forth. At noon, too exhausted to eat, I lay down in a corner to rest, but before my aching muscles had stopped throbbing the afternoon work began and the foreman was calling to me to hurry.

My head ached with a queer jumping pain and I was so dizzy that I dropped a tray of bottles and blundered into the edge of the door more than once, but I shut my teeth tight and kept on. I did not mean to lose that job. It meant nearly two dollars a week.

I kept at it till late that afternoon, dripping with perspiration while my teeth chattered and my legs grew more unsteady with every trip. Then, as I bent before a furnace to pick up a tray there was a sudden glare of light and heat, a tremendous, crashing explosion. Everything swirled into flame and then into darkness.

When I came to myself again I was in an infirmary bed, just a mass of burning pain

160

wrapped in bandages, and I heard myself saying vigorously, while some tried to quiet me, "I am the greatest actor in London. I tell you I am the greatest actor in London."

CHAPTER XXI

In which I encounter the inexorable rules of a London hospital, causing much consternation; fight a battle with pride; and unexpectedly enter an upsetting situation.

I DID not find the hospital unpleasant, for I had enough to eat there, and although my burns were painful, it was a delight to be in a clean bed. I lay there three weeks, quite contented, and all day long, and when I could not sleep at night, I thought over my stage experience and the mistakes I had made in it and finally grew able to laugh at myself. It is the only, valuable thing I have ever learned.

Life trips people up and makes them fall on their noses at every step. It takes the very qualities that make success and turns them into stumbling blocks, and when we go tumbling over them the only thing to do is to get up and laugh at ourselves. If I had not been a precocious, self-satisfied, egotistic boy, able to imagine unreal things and think them true, I could never have been a success on the stage,

162

and if I had been none of those things I would not have thrown away the opportunity Mrs. Kendall gave me and been a failure. That is an Irish bull, but life must have its little joke, and there you are.

At the end of the three weeks my burns were sufficiently healed, and one day the nurse came and told me that I could leave the hospital.

"Very well," I said, "but how? I have no clothes."

"My goodness!" she said. "I—but you can't stay here, you know."

"Will you lend me a sheet?" I asked. "I must wear something."

"Oh, no; we couldn't do that," she replied, and went away, dazed by the problem. I lay there grinning to myself and ate my supper with good appetite. The next day the doctor came and looked at me and scratched his head and said testily that I was well enough to go and must go; I must get some clothes.

"How can I get clothes unless I go and earn them, and how can I earn them if I don't have any?" I asked him.

"Isn't there any way to get this lad any clothes?" he said to the nurse. She said she did

163

not know, there had never been a case just like it before. She would ask the superintendent. She came back with the superintendent, and all three of them looked at me. The superintendent said firmly that I must go, that it was against the rules for me to stay any longer. I replied firmly that I would not go into the streets of London without any clothes. The superintendent shut her lips firmly and went away.

There was a great sensation in the hospital. My own garments had been destroyed in the explosion. The rules demanded that I go, but the rules provided no clothes for me; I would not go without clothes, and no one could feel my position unreasonable. The hospital swayed under the strain of the situation.

The next afternoon a representative of the Society for the Relief of the Deserving Poor called to see me. She asked a dozen questions, wrote the answers in a book and went away. Another day passed. The nurses were pale with suspense. No clothes arrived.

Wild rumors circulated that I was to be wrapped in a blanket and set out in the night, but they were contradicted by the fact that the rules did not provide for the loan of the blanket. Friendly patients urged me to be firm, kindly nurses told me not to worry, the superintendent was reported baffled by the rules of the charitable organizations, which did not provide for clothing patients in the charity hospitals.

Some natural resentment was felt against me for not fitting any rules, but the food came regularly and I ate and slept comfortably. On the fourth day, when it was felt that something desperate must be done, the situation suddenly cleared. Sidney arrived.

The representative of the S. R. D. P. had called at my mother's address in the course of her investigations as to my worthiness and found him there. He was playing in an East End theater and very much worried about my disappearance. On hearing of my plight he had hastened to the rescue and cut short my life of ease and plenty under the unwilling shelter of the hospital rules. He brought me clothes, and I departed, to the disappointment of the other patients who felt it an anti-climax.

Well fed and rested, and with the stimulus of Sidney's encouragement, I started again my search for a part. Much as I had hated the

Strand at times, it was like coming home again to be tramping up and down the agents' stairs and exchanging boasts with the other actors while I waited in the outer offices. Usually I waited long hours, only to be sent away at last with the office boy's curt announcement that the agent would see no one, and when sometimes I did penetrate into the inner offices I met always the same, "Nothing in sight. Things are very quiet just now. Drop in again." Then I came out, with my old jaunty air hiding my bitter disappointment and tramped down the stairs and along the Strand and up to another office, to wait again.

Mrs. Dobbs, my mother's landlady, moved to Sweetbay, and being fond of my mother and her sweet gentle ways, had consented to take her there for a moderate rate. Sidney and I lived together in a bed-sitting-room in Alfred Place on very scant fare and I hated to face him at night.

"Well, any news?" he always asked, pleasantly enough, but I dreaded the moment and having to say, "No, not yet." It hurt my pride terribly, and after several months of it the misery of that first moment of meeting Sidney drove me into hurting my pride even more in another way.

"Look here, what's all this talk about playing lead and being with William Gillette worth to you?" an agent said to me one day. "You'll take anything you can jolly well get, no matter what it is, won't you? Well, Dailey, over at the Grand, is putting out a comedy next week with *Casey's Circus*. There's fifteen parts, none of 'em cast yet. Go and see what you can do."

I came out of his office in an agony of indecision, for while it was true that I had said to myself many times that I would take any part I could get, I had never imagined myself acting in *Casey's Circus*. All the pride that had survived those months of discouragement writhed at the idea—I who had been a hit in a West End theater acting a low vulgar comedy in dirty fourth-rate houses—why, it was not so good a chance as my part in *Rags to Riches!* I said savagely that I would not do it. Then I thought of Sidney and bit my lips and hesitated.

In the end, burning with shame and resentment, I went to see Dailey. At least a hundred third-rate actors packed the stairs to his office and more were blocking the street and sitting on the curbs before his door opened. I was crushed in the crowd of them, smothered by rank perfume and the close thick air of the dirty stairs, and I hated myself and the situation more every minute of the three hours I waited there, but I stayed, half hoping he would not give me a part. At least I could feel then that I had done all I could.

At last my turn came. I straightened my hat, squared my shoulders and marched in, determined to be very haughty and dignified. Mr. Dailey, a fat red-faced man, with his waistcoat unbuttoned, sat by a desk chewing a big cigar.

"Mr. Dailey," I said, "I——" I don't know how it happened. My foot slipped. I tried to straighten up, slipped again, fell on all fours over a chair, which fell over on me, and sat up on the floor with the chair in my lap. "——want a part," I finished, furious.

Mr. Dailey howled and laughed and choked, and held his sides and laughed again and choked, purple in the face.

"You'll do," he said at last. "Great

entrance! Great! Ten shillings a week and railway fares; what do you say to that, my lad?"

"I won't take it," I retorted.

CHAPTER XXII

In which I attempt to be serious and am funny instead; seize the opportunity to get a raise in pay; and again consider coming to America.

MR. DAILEY would not let me go, but, still wiping tears of laughter from his eyes, began shilling by shilling to raise his offer. My entirely unintentional comedy entrance had pleased him mightily, and indeed, as soon as I saw he took it as a deliberate effort on my part, I began to be not a little proud of it myself. It was not every one, I said to myself, who could fall over a chair so comically as that!

Cheered and emboldened by this reflection, I drove a shrewd bargain, and at last, persuaded by the offer of a pound a week and a long engagement if I could keep on being funny, I consented to become a member of *Casey's Circus,* and returned whistling to our lodgings, able to face Sidney with some degree of pride because I had an engagement at last.

170

We began rehearsals next day in a very dirty dark room over a public house—fifteen ragged, hungry-looking, sallow-faced boys desperately being funny under the direction of a fat greasy-looking manager who smelled strongly of ale. It was difficult work for me at first. Being funny is at best a hard job, and being funny in those conditions, which I heartily detested, seemed at first almost impossible. More than once, when the manager swore at me more than usual, I felt like throwing the whole thing up and would have done so but for the dread of going back to the endless tramping up and down the Strand and being a burden on Sidney.

Casey's Circus was putting on that season a burlesque of persons in the public eye, and I was cast for the part of Doctor Body, a patent-medicine faker, who was drawing big crowds on the London street corners and selling a specific for all the ills of man and beast at a shilling the bottle. Watching him one afternoon, I was seized with a great idea. I would let the manager rehearse me all he jolly well liked, but when the opening night came I would play Doctor Body as he really was—I

171

would put on such a marvelous character delineation that even the lowest music-hall audience would recognize it as great acting and I would be rescued by some good manager and brought back to a West End theater.

The idea grew upon me. Despising with all my heart the cheap, clap-trap burlesque which the manager tried to drill into me, I paid only enough attention to it to get through rehearsals somehow, hurrying out afterward to watch Doctor Body and to practise before the mirror in our lodgings my own idea of the part. I felt that I did it well and thrilled with pride at the thought of playing it soon with the eye of a great manager upon me.

The night of the opening came and I hurried to the dirty makeshift dressing-room in a cheap East End music-hall with all the sensations of a boy committing his first burglary. I must manage to make up as the real Doctor Body and to get on the stage before I was caught. Once on the stage, without the burlesque make-up which I was supposed to wear, I knew I could make the part go. I painted my face stealthily among the uproar and quarrels of the other fourteen boys, who were

172

"Can you beat it?"

all in the same dressing-room fighting over the mirrors and hurling epithets and make-up boxes at one another.

The air tingled with excitement. The distracted manager, thrusting his head in at the door, cried with oaths that Casey himself was in front and he'd stand for no nonsense. We could hear him rushing away, swearing at the scene shifters, who had made some error in placing the set. The audience was in bad humor; we could faintly hear it hooting and whistling. It had thrown rotten fruit at the act preceding ours. In the confusion I managed to make up and to get into my clothes, troubled by the size of the high hat I was to wear, which came down over my ears. I stuffed it with paper to keep it at the proper angle on my head, and trembling with nervousness, but sure of myself when I should get on the stage, I stole out of the dressing-room and stationed myself in the darkest part of the wings.

The boy who appeared first was having a bad time of it, missing his cues and being hissed and hooted by the audience. The manager rushed up to me, caught sight of my make-up and stopped aghast.

173

" 'Ere, you can't go on like that!" he said in a furious whisper, catching my arm.

"Let me alone; I know what I'm doing!" I cried angrily, wrenching myself from him. My great plan was not to be spoiled now at the last minute. The manager reached for me again, purple with wrath, but, quick as an eel, I ducked under his arm, seized the cane I was to carry and rushed on to the stage half a minute too soon.

Once in the glare of the footlights I dropped into the part, determined to play it, play it well, and hold the audience. The other boy, whose part I had spoiled, confused by my unexpected appearance, stammered in his lines and fell back. I advanced slowly, impressively, feeling the gaze of the crowd, and, with a carefully studied gesture, hung my cane—I held it by the wrong end! Instead of hanging on my arm, as I expected, it clattered on the stage. Startled, I stooped to pick it up, and my high silk hat fell from my head. I grasped it, put it on quickly, and, paper wadding falling out, I found my whole head buried in its black depths.

A great burst of laughter came from the

audience. When, pushing the hat back, I went desperately on with my serious lines, the crowd roared, held its sides, shrieked with mirth till it gasped. The more serious I was, the funnier it struck the audience. I came off at last, pursued by howls of laughter and wild applause, which called me back again. I had made the hit of the evening.

"That was a good bit of business, my lad," Mr. Casey himself said, coming behind the scenes and meeting me in the wings when finally the audience let me leave the stage the second time. "Your idea?"

"Oh, certainly," I replied airily. "Not bad, I flatter myself—er—but of course not what I might do at that." And, seizing the auspicious moment, I demanded a raise to two pounds a week and got it.

The next week I was headlined as "Charles Chaplin, the funniest actor in London," and *Casey's Circus* packed the house wherever it was played. I had stumbled on the secret of being funny—unexpectedly. An idea, going in one direction, meets an opposite idea suddenly. "Ha! Ha!" you shriek. It works every time.

175

I walk on to the stage, serious, dignified, solemn, pause before an easy chair, spread my coat-tails with an elegant gesture—and sit on the cat. Nothing funny about it, really, especially if you consider the feelings of the cat. But you laugh. You laugh because it is unexpected. Those little nervous shocks make you laugh; you can't help it. Peeling onions makes you weep, and seeing a fat man carrying a custard pie slip and sit down on it makes you laugh.

In the two years I was with *Casey's Circus* I gradually gave up my idea of playing great parts on the dramatic stage. I grew to like the comedy work, to enjoy hearing the bursts of laughter from the audience, and getting the crowd in good humor and keeping it so was a nightly frolic for me. Then, too, by degrees all my old self-confidence and pride came back, with the difference, indeed, that I did not take them too seriously, as before, but merely felt them like a pleasant inner warmth as I walked on the Strand and saw the envious looks of other actors not so fortunate.

One day, walking there in this glow of success, swinging my cane with a nonchalant air and humming to myself, I met the old comedian who had been with the *Rags to Riches* company.

"I say, old top," he said eagerly, falling into step with me, "do a chap a favor, won't you now? There's a big chance with Carno—I have it on the quiet he's planning to take a company to America, and half a dozen parts not cast. Good pickings, what? I can't get a word with the beggar, but he'd listen to you. See what you can do for yourself and then say a good word for me, won't you, what?"

CHAPTER XXIII

In which I startle a promoter; dream a great triumph in the land of skyscrapers and buffalo; and wait long for a message.

AMERICA! Fred Carno!

The words went off like rockets in my mind, bursting into thousands of sparkling ideas. Fred Carno, the biggest comedy producer in London—a man who could by a word make me the best-known comedian in Europe! I could already see the press notices—"Charlie Chaplin, the great comedian, in the spectacular Carno production—." And America, that strange country across the sea, where I had heard men thought no more of half-crowns than we thought of six-pences; New York, where the buildings were ten, twenty, even thirty floors high, and the sky blazed with enormous signs in electric light; Chicago, where the tinned meat came from, and, between, vast plains covered with buffalo and wild forests, where, as the train plunged through them at tremendous speed, I might

178

see from the compartment window the American red men around their camp-fires! The man at my side was saying that there was a chance to go to America with Carno!

"Go see him, old chap; please do," the old comedian begged me. "He'll see you, quick enough, though he keeps me waiting in his offices like a dog. And say a good word for me; just get me a chance to see him. I've put you on to a good thing, what? You won't forget old friends, will you now?"

"Er—certainly not, certainly not!" I assured him loftily. "Now I think of it, Freddie was mentioning to me the other day something about sending a company to America. Next time I see him—the very next time, on my word—I'll mention your name. You can depend on it."

Then, waving away his fervid thanks and declining kindly his suggestion to have a glass of bitters, I hailed a cab and drove away, eager to be alone and think over the dazzling prospect. My own small success seemed flat enough beside it. America—Fred Carno! After all, why not? I asked myself. I could make people laugh; Carno did not have a man who could do it better. Just let me have a chance to show him what I could do!

So excited that I could feel the blood beating in my temples and every nerve quivering, I beat on the cab window with my cane and called to the driver to take me to Carno's offices quick. "An extra shilling if you do it in five minutes!" I cried, and sat on the edge of the seat as the cab lurched and swayed, hoping only that I could get there before all the parts were gone.

I walked into Carno's offices with a quick assured step, hiding my excitement under an air of haughty importance, though only a great effort kept my hand from trembling as I gave my card to the office boy. I swallowed hard and called to mind all the press notices I had received in the two years with *Casey's Circus* while I waited, trying to gain an assurance I did not feel, for Carno was a very big man, indeed. When the office boy returned and ushered me into the inner office I felt my knees unsteady under me.

"Ah, you got here quickly," Mr. Carno said pleasantly, waving me to a chair, and this unexpected reception completed my confusion.

"Oh, yes. I was—I happened to be going by," I replied, dazed.

Mr. Carno leaned back in his chair, carefully fitting his finger tips together and looked at me keenly with his lips pursed up. I said nothing more, being doubtful just what to say, and after a minute he sat up very briskly and spoke.

"As I mentioned in my note," he began, and the office seemed to explode into fireworks about me. He had sent me a note. He wanted me, then. I could make my own terms. "And perhaps I could use you for next season," he finished whatever he had said.

"Yes," I said promptly. "In your American company."

"My American company? Well, no. That is still very indefinite," he replied. "But I can give you a good part with *Repairs* in the provinces. Thirty weeks, at three pounds."

"No, I would not consider that," I answered firmly. "I will take a part in your American company at six pounds." *Six* pounds—it was an enormous salary; twice as much as I had ever received. I was aghast as I heard the words, but I said doggedly to myself that I would stand by them. I was a great comedian; Fred Carno himself had sent for me; I was worth six pounds.

"*Six* pounds! It's unheard of. I never pay it," Mr. Carno said sharply.

"Six pounds, not a farthing less," I insisted.

"In that case I am afraid I can't use you. Good morning," he answered.

"Good morning," I said, and rising promptly I left the office.

That night I played as I had never played before. The audience howled with laughter from my entrance till my last exit and recalled me again and again, until I would only bow and back off. I carried in a pocket of my stage clothes the note from Mr. Carno, which I had found waiting at the theater, and I winked at myself triumphantly in the mirror while I took off my make-up.

"He'll come around. Watch me!" I said confidently, and not even Sidney's misgivings nor his repeated urgings to seize the chance with Carno at any salary could shake my determination.

"I'm going to America," I said firmly. "And I won't go under six pounds. Living

182

costs terrifically over there; all the lodgings have built-in baths and they charge double for it. I stand by six pounds and I'll get it, never fear."

In my own heart I had misgivings more than once in the months that followed without another message from Carno, but I set my teeth and vowed that, since I had said six pounds, six pounds it should be. And I worked at comedy effects all day long in our lodgings, falling over chairs and tripping over my cane for hours together, till I was black and blue, but prepared, when the curtain went up at night, to make the audience hold their sides and shriek helplessly with tears of laughter on their cheeks.

"Any news?" Sidney began to ask again every evening, but I managed always to say, "Not yet!" with cocky assurance. "He'll send for me, never fear," I said, warmed with the thought of the applause I was getting and the press notices.

The season with *Casey's Circus* was ending and I took care not to let any hint of my intention to leave reach the ears of the manager, but I refused to believe that I would be obliged to fall back on him. I looked eagerly every day for another note from Carno.

"Don't worry, I'll see you get your bit when the time is ripe," I told the old comedian whenever he importuned me for news, as he did frequently. "You know how it is, old top —you have to manage these big men just right."

At last the note came. It reached me at my lodgings early one morning, having been sent on from the theater, and I trembled with excitement while I dressed. I forced myself to eat breakfast slowly and to idle about a bit before starting for Carno's offices, not to reach them too early and appear too eager, but when at last I set out the cab seemed to do no more than crawl.

"Well, I find I can use you in the American company," Mr. Carno said.

"Very well," I replied nonchalantly.

"And—er—as to salary—," he began, but I cut in.

"Salary?" I said, shrugging my shoulders. "Why mention it? We went over that before," and I waved my hand carelessly. "Six pounds," I said airily.

184

He looked at me a minute, frowning. Then he laughed.

"All right, confound you!" he said, smiling, and took out the contract.

Three weeks later, booked for a solid year in the United States, looking forward to playing on the Keith circuit among the Eastern sky-scrapers and on the Orpheum circuit in the Wild West among the American red men, I stood on the deck of a steamer and saw the rugged sky-line of New York rising from the sea.

CHAPTER XXIV

In which I discover many strange things in that strange land, America; visit San Francisco for the first time; and meet an astounding reception in the offices of a cinematograph company.

Now, since I was twenty at the time, four years ago, when I stood on the deck of the steamer and saw America rising into view on the horizon, it may seem strange to some persons that I had no truer idea of this country than to suppose just west of New York a wild country inhabited by American Indians and traversed by great herds of buffalo. It is natural enough, however, when one reflects that I had spent nearly all my life in London, which is, like all great cities, a most narrow-minded and provincial place, and that my only schooling had been the little my mother was able to give me, combined later with much eager reading of romances. Fenimore Cooper, your own American writer, had pictured for me this country as it was a hundred years ago, and what

186

English boy would suppose a whole continent could be made over in a short hundred years?

So, while the steamer docked, I stood quivering with eagerness to be off into the wonders of that forest of skyscrapers which is New York, with all the sensations of a boy transported to Mars, or any other unknown world, where anything might happen. Indeed, one of the strangest things—to my way of thinking—which I encountered in the New World, was brought to my attention a moment after I landed. At the very foot of the gangplank Mr. Reeves, the manager of the American company, who was with me, was halted by a very fat little man, richly dressed, who rushed up and grasped him enthusiastically by both hands.

"Velgome! Velgome to our gountry!" he cried. "How are you, Reeves? How goes it?"

Mr. Reeves replied in a friendly manner, and the little man turned to me inquiringly. "Who's the kid?" he asked.

"This is Mr. Chaplin, our leading comedian," Mr. Reeves said, while I bristled at the word "kid." The fat man, I found, was Marcus Loew, a New York theatrical producer. He shook hands with me warmly and asked immediately, "Vell, and vot do you think of our gountry, young man?"

"I have never been in Berlin," I said stiffly. "I have never cared to go there," I added rudely, resenting his second reference to my youth.

"I mean America. How do you like America? This is our gountry now. We're all Americans together over here!" Marcus Loew said with real enthusiasm in his voice, and I drew myself up in haughty surprise. "My word, this *is* a strange country," I said to myself. Foreigners, and all that, calling themselves citizens! This is going rather far, even for a republic, even for America, where anything might happen.

That was the thing which most impressed me for weeks. Germans, it seemed, and English and Irish and French and Italians and Poles, all mixed up together, all one nation— it seemed incredible to me, like something against all the laws of nature. I went about in a continual wonder at it. Not even the high buildings, higher even than I had imagined, nor the enormous, flaming electric signs on

Broadway, nor the high, hysterical, shrill sound of the street traffic, so different from the heavy roar of London, was so strange to me as this mixing of races. Indeed, it was months before I could become accustomed to it, and months more before I saw how good it is, and felt glad to be part of such a nation myself.

We were playing a sketch called *A Night in a London Music-Hall,* which probably many people still remember. I was cast for the part of a drunken man, who furnished most of the comedy, and the sketch proved to be a great success, so that I played that one part continuously for over two years, traveling from coast to coast with it twice.

The number of American cities seemed endless to me, like the little bores the Chinese make, one inside the other, so that it seems no matter how many you take out, there are still more inside. I had imagined this country a broad wild continent, dotted sparsely with great cities —New York, Chicago, San Francisco—with wide distances between. The distances were there, as I expected, but there seemed no end to the cities. New York, Buffalo, Pittsburgh, Cincinnati, Columbus, Indianapolis, Chicago,

St. Louis, Kansas City, Omaha, Denver—and San Francisco not even in sight yet! No Indians, either.

Toward the end of the summer we reached San Francisco the first time, very late, because the train had lost time over the mountains, so that there was barely time for us to reach the Orpheum and make up in time for the first performance. My stage hat was missing, there was a wild search for it, while we held the curtain and the house grew a little impatient, but we could not find it anywhere. At last I seized a high silk hat from the outraged head of a man who had come behind the scenes to see Reeves and rushed on to the stage. The hat was too loose. Every time I tried to speak a line it fell off, and the audience went into ecstasies. It was one of the best hits of the season, that hat.

It slid back down my neck, and the audience laughed; it fell over my nose, and they howled; I picked it up on the end of my cane, looked at it stupidly and tried to put the cane on my head, and they roared. I do not know the feelings of its owner, who for a time stood glaring at me from the wings, for when at last, after

190

the third curtain call, I came off holding the much dilapidated hat in my hands, he had gone. Bareheaded, I suppose, and probably still very angry.

After the show I came out on the street into a cold gray fog, which blurred the lights and muffled the sound of my steps on the damp pavement, and, drawing great breaths of it into my lungs, I was happy. "For the lova Mike!" I said to Reeves, being very proud of my American slang. "This is a little bit of all right, what? Just like home, don't you know! What do you know about that!" And I felt that, next to London, I liked San Francisco, and was sorry we were to stay only two weeks.

We returned to New York, playing return dates on the "big time" circuits, and I almost regretted the close of the season and the return to London. The night we closed at Keith's I found a message waiting for me at the theater.

"We want you in the pictures. Come and see me and talk it over. Mack Sennett."

"Who's Mack Sennett?" I asked Reeves,

and he told me he was with the Keystone motion-picture company. "Oh, the cinematographs!" I said, for I knew them in London, and regarded them as even lower than the music-halls. I tore up the note and threw it away.

"I suppose we're going home next week?" I asked Reeves, and he said he thought not; the "little big time" circuits wanted us and he was waiting for a cable from Carno.

Early next day I called at his apartments, eager to learn what he had heard, for I wanted very much to stay in America another year, and saw no way to do it if Carno recalled the company. I did not think again of the note from Sennett, for I did not regard seriously an offer to go into the cinematographs. I was delighted to hear that we were going to stay, and left New York in great spirits, with the prospect of another year with *A Night in a London Music-Hall* in America.

Twelve months later, back in New York again, I received another message from Mr. Sennett, to which I paid no more attention than to the first one. We were sailing for London the following month. One day, while I was walking down Broadway with a chance acquaintance, we passed the Keystone offices and my companion asked me to come in with him. He had some business with a man there. I went in, and was waiting in the outer office when Mr. Sennett came through and recognized me.

"Good morning, Mr. Chaplin, glad to see you! Come right in," he said cordially, and, ashamed to tell him I had not come in reply to his message, that indeed I had not meant to answer it at all, I followed him into his private office. I talked vaguely, waiting for an opportunity to get away without appearing rude. At last I saw it.

"Let's not beat about the bush any longer," Mr. Sennett said. "What salary will you take to come with the Keystone?" This was my chance to end the interview, and I grasped it eagerly.

"Two hundred dollars a week," I said, naming the most extravagant price which came into my head.

"All right," he replied promptly. "When can you start?"

CHAPTER XXV

In which I find that the incredible has happened;
burn my bridges behind me and penetrate for
the first time the mysterious regions behind the
moving-picture film.

"But—I said two hundred dollars a week," I
repeated feebly, stunned by Mr. Sennett's unexpected response. Two hundred dollars a
week—forty pounds—he couldn't mean it! It
was absolutely impossible.

"Yes. That's right. Two hundred dollars
a week," Mr. Sennett said crisply. "When can
you begin work?"

"Why—you know, I must have a two-years'
contract at that salary," I said, feeling my
way carefully, for I still could not credit this
as a genuine offer.

"All right, we'll fix it up. Two years, two
hundred—" he made a little memorandum on
a desk pad, and something in the matter-of-
fact way he did it convinced me that this incredible thing had actually happened. "Contract will be ready this afternoon, say at four

194

Mack Sennett

o'clock. That will suit you? And we'd like you to start for California as soon as possible."

"Certainly. Oh, of course," I said, though still more confounded by this, for I did not see the connection between California and the cinematograph. More than anything else, however, I felt that I needed air and an opportunity to consider where I stood anyway, and what I was going to do.

I walked down Broadway in a daze. An actor for a cinematographic company—my mind shied at the thought. How were the confounded things made, anyhow? Still, two hundred dollars a week—what would happen if I could not do the work? I tried to imagine what it would be like. Acting before a machine—how could I tell whether I was funny or not? The machine would not laugh. Then suddenly I stopped short in a tangle of cross-street traffic and cried aloud, "Look here, you could have got twice the money!" But instantly that thought was swept away again by my speculations about the work and my concern as to whether or not I could do it.

At four o'clock I returned to the Keystone offices, in a mood between exultation and panic, and signed the contract, beginning with a feeble scratch of the pen, but ending in a bold black scrawl. It was done; I was a moving-picture actor, and heaven only knew what would happen next!

"Can you start for California to-night?" Mr. Sennett asked, while he blotted the contract.

"I can start any time," I said a little uncertainly. "But shouldn't I rehearse first?"

He laughed. "You don't rehearse moving pictures in advance. You do that as they are being taken," he replied. "They'll show you all that at the studios. You'll soon catch on, and you'll photograph all right, don't worry."

Still with some misgivings, but becoming more jubilant every moment, I hurried away to get my luggage and to announce to Mr. Reeves that I was not going back to London with Carno's company. He began to urge me to change my mind, to wait while he could cable to Carno and get me an offer from him for the next season, but I triumphantly produced my contract, and after one look at the figures he was dumb.

"Two hundred dollars—Holy Moses!" he

196

managed to ejaculate after a moment, and I chuckled at the thought of Mr. Carno's face when he should hear the news.

"It's not so bad, for a beginning," I said modestly, trying my best to speak as though it were but a trifle, but unable to keep the exultation out of my voice. A dozen times, in the hurry of arranging my affairs and catching the train, I stopped to look at the contract again, half fearful that the figures might have changed.

My high spirits lasted until I was settled in the Chicago Limited, pulling out of New York with a great noise of whistles and bells, and steaming away into the darkness toward California and the unknown work of a moving-picture actor. Then misgivings came upon me in a cloud. I saw myself trying to be funny before the cold eye of a machine, unable to speak my lines, not helped by any applause, failing miserably. How could I give the effect of ripping my trousers without the "r-r-r-r-r-rip!" of a snare-drum? When I slipped and fell on my head, how could the audience get the point without the loud hollow "boom!" from the orchestra?

197

Every added mile farther from London increased my doubts, hard as I tried to encourage myself with thoughts of my past successes. Moving-picture work was different, and if I should fail in California I would be a long, long way from home.

I reached Los Angeles late at night, very glad that I would not have to report at the Keystone studios until morning. I tried to oversleep next day, but it was impossible; I ,was awake long before dawn. I dressed as slowly as possible, wandered about the streets as long as I could, and finally ordered an enormous breakfast, choosing the most expensive café I could find, because the more expensive the place the longer one must wait to be served, and I was seizing every pretext for delay. When the food came I could not eat it, and suddenly I said to myself that I was behaving like a child; I would hurry to the studios and get it over. I rushed from the café, called a taxi and bribed the chauffeur to break the speed laws and get me there quick.

When I alighted before the studio, a big new building of bright unpainted wood, I took a deep breath, gripped my cane firmly, walked briskly to the door—and hurried past it. I walked a block or. so, calling myself names, before I could bring myself to turn and come back. At last, with the feeling that I was dragging myself by the collar, I managed to get up the steps and push open the door.

I was welcomed with a cordiality that restored a little of my self-confidence. The director of the company in which I was to star had been informed of my arrival by telegraph and was waiting for me on the stage, they said. An office boy, whistling cheerfully, volunteered to take me to him, and, leading me through the busy offices, opened the stage door.

A glare of light and heat burst upon me. The stage, a yellow board floor covering at least two blocks, lay in a blaze of sunlight, intensified by dozens of white canvas reflectors stretched overhead. On it was a wilderness of "sets"—drawing-rooms, prison interiors, laundries, balconies, staircases, caves, fire-escapes, kitchens, cellars. Hundreds of actors were strolling about in costume; carpenters were hammering away at new sets; five companies were playing before five clicking cameras. There was a roar of confused sound—screams, laughs, an explosion, shouted commands, pounding, whistling, the bark of a dog. The air was thick with the smell of new lumber in the sun, flash-light powder, cigarette smoke.

The director was standing in his shirt-sleeves beside a clicking camera, holding a mass of manuscript in his hand and clenching an unlighted cigar between his teeth. He was barking short commands to the company which was playing—"To the left; to the left, Jim! There, hold it! Smile, Maggie! That's right. Good! Look out for the lamp!"

The scene over, he welcomed me cordially enough, but hurriedly.

"Glad to see you. How soon can you go to work? This afternoon? Good! Two o'clock, if you can make it. Look around the studio a bit, if you like. Sorry I haven't a minute to spare; I'm six hundred feet short this week, and they're waiting for the film. G'by. Two o'clock, sharp!" Then he turned away and cried, "All ready for the next scene. Basement interior," and was hard at work again.

CHAPTER XXVI

In which I see a near-tragedy which is a comedy on
the films; meet my fellow actors, the red and blue
rats; and prepare to fall through a trap-door with
a pie.

THE little self-confidence I had been able to
muster failed me entirely when the director dismissed me so crisply. The place was so strange
to my experience, every one of the hundreds
of persons about me was so absorbed in his
work, barely glancing at me as I passed, that
I felt helpless and out of place there. Still,
the studio was crowded with interesting things
to see, and I determined to remain and learn
all I could of this novel business of producing
cinema film before my own turn came to do
it. So I assumed an air of dignity, marred
somewhat by the fact that my collar was beginning to wilt and my nose burning red in
the hot sunlight, and strolled down the stage
behind the clicking cameras.

At a little distance I saw the front of a three-
story tenement, built of brick, with windows

201

and fire-escape all complete, looking quite natural in front, but supported by wooden scaffolding behind. Near it, on a high platform, was a big camera, and a man with a shade over his eyes busy adjusting it, and a dozen men were stretching a net such as acrobats use. A number of actors were hurrying in that direction, and I joined them, eager to see what was to happen.

"What's all the row?" I asked a girl in the costume of a nurse, who stood eating a sandwich, the only idle person in sight.

"Scene in a new comedy," she answered pleasantly but indifferently.

"Ah, yes. That's in my own line," I said importantly. "I am Charles Chaplin."

She looked at me, and I saw that she had never heard of me.

"You're a comedian?" she inquired.

"Yes," I answered sharply. "Er—do you go on in this?"

"Oh, no. I'm not an actress," she said, surprised. "I'm here professionally." I did not understand what she meant. "In case of accidents," she explained, plainly thinking me stupid. "Sometimes nothing happens, but you

202

never can tell. Eight men were pretty badly
hurt in the explosion in the comedy they put
on last week," she finished brightly.

I felt a cold sensation creep up my spine.

In the "set" before us there was a great bustle of preparation. A long light ladder was
set up at a sharp angle, firmly fastened at the
bottom, but with the upper end unsupported,
quivering in the air.

Men were running about shouting directions
and questions. Suddenly, balancing precari-
ously on the narraw platform behind the camera operator, the director appeared and clapped
his hands sharply. "All ready down there?"
he called.

"All ready!" some one yelled in reply.

"Let 'er go!"

The windows in the brick wall burst out-
ward with a loud explosion and swirling clouds
of smoke. Up the swaying ladder ran a po-
liceman and at the same instant, caught up
by invisible wires, another man soared through
the air and met him. On the top rung of the
ladder they balanced, clutching each other.

"Fight! Fight! Put some life into it!"
yelled the director. "Turn on the water, Jim!"

My eyes straining in their sockets, I saw the two men in the air slugging each other desperately, while the ladder bent beneath them. Then from the ground a two-inch stream of water rose and struck them—held there, playing on them while they struggled.

"Great! Great! Keep it up!" the director howled. "More smoke!" Another explosion answered him; through the eddying smoke I could see the two men still fighting, while the stream from the hose played on them.

"Let go now. Fall! Fall! I tell you, fall!" the director shouted. The two men lurched, the wires gave way, and, falling backward, sheer, from a height of twenty-five feet, the comedian dropped and struck the net. The net broke.

The scene broke up in a panic. The nurse ran through the crowd, a stretcher appeared, and on it the comedian was carried past me, followed by the troubled director and a physician. "Not serious, merely shock; he'll be all right to-morrow," the physician was saying, but I felt my knees shaking under me.

"So *this* is the life of a cinema comedian!" I thought, breathing hard.

I did not feel hungry, some way, and besides, I felt that if I left the studio for luncheon I would probably be unable to bring myself back again, so I picked out the coolest place I could find and sat down to await two o'clock. I was in a dim damp "basement set," furnished only with an overturned box, on which I sat. After a time a strange scratching noise attracted my attention, and looking down I saw a procession of bright red and blue rats coming out between my feet. I leaped from the box with my hair on end and left, saying nothing to any one.

At two o'clock, quivering with nervousness, I presented myself to the director. He was brisk and hurried as before and plunged immediately into a description of the part I was to play, pausing only to mop his perspiring forehead now and then. The heat had increased; under the reflectors the place was like a furnace, but my spine was still cold with apprehension.

"Is it an acrobatic part?" I asked, as soon as I could force myself to inquire.

"No, not this one. You're a hungry tramp in the country. We'll take the interiors here, and for the rest we'll go out on 'location,'" the director answered, ruffling the pages of the "working script" of the play. "We'll do the last scene first—basement set. Let's run through it now; then you can make up and we'll get it on the film before the light's gone."

He led the way to the basement set and began to instruct me how to play the part.

"You fall in, down the trap-door," he said. "Pick yourself up, slowly, and register surprise. Don't look at the camera, of course. You have a pie under your coat. Take it out, begin to eat it. Register extreme hunger. Then you hear a noise, start, set down the pie, and peer out through the grating. When you turn around the rats will be eating the pie. Get it?"

I said I did, and while the director peered through the camera lens I rehearsed as well as I could. I had to do it over and over, because each time I forgot and got out of the range of the camera lens. At last, however, with the aid of a five-foot circle of dots on the floor, I did it passably well, and was sent to make up in one of dozens of dressing-rooms, built in a long row beside the stage. My costume, supplied by the Keystone wardrobe, was ready, and I was reassured by the sight of it and the make-up box. Here at last was something I was quite familiar with, and I produced a make-up of which I was proud.

When I returned to the stage the camera operator was waiting, and a small crowd of actors and carpenters had gathered to watch the scene. The director was inspecting the colored rats and giving orders to have their tails repainted—quick, because the blamed things had licked the color off and would register tailless. A stage hand was standing by with a large pie in his hand.

"Ready, Chaplin?" the director called, and then he looked at me.

"Holy Moses, where did you get that makeup?" he asked in astonishment, and every one stared. "That won't do; that won't do at all. Look at your skin, man; it will register gray —and those lines—you can't use lines like that in the pictures. Roberts, go show him how to make up."

I thought of my first appearance in *Rags to Riches,* and felt almost as humiliated as I had then, while Roberts went with me to the dressing-room and showed me how to coat my face and neck with a dull brick-brown paint, and to load my lashes heavily with black. The character lines I had drawn with such care would not do in the pictures, I learned, because they would show as lines. I must give the character effect by the muscles of my face.

Feeling very strange in this make-up, I went back the second time to the stage. The director, satisfied this time, gave me a few last directions and the pie, and I mounted to the top of the set.

"Remember, don't look at the camera, keep within range, throw yourself into the part and say anything that comes into your head," the director said. "All ready? Go to it."

The camera began to click; I clutched the pie, took a long breath, and tumbled through the trap-door.

CHAPTER XXVII

In which, much against my will, I eat three cherry
pies; see myself for the first time on a moving-
picture screen and discover that I am a hopeless
failure on the films.

"REGISTER surprise! Register surprise!" the
director ordered in a low tense voice, while I
struggled to get up without damaging the pie.
I turned my head toward the clicking camera,
and suddenly it seemed like a great eye watching me. I gazed into the round black lens,
and it seemed to swell until it was yards across.
I tried to pull my face into an expression of
surprise, but the muscles were stiff and I could
only stare fascinated at the lens. The clicking
stopped.

"Too bad. You looked at the camera. Try
it again," said the director, making a note of
the number of feet of film spoiled. He was
a very patient director; he stopped the camera
and placed the pie on top of it for safety, while
I fell through the trap-door twice and twice
played the scene through, using the pie tin.

Then the pie was placed under my coat again, the camera began to click, and again I started the scene. But the clicking drew my attention to the lens in spite of myself. I managed to keep from looking directly at it, but I felt that my acting was stiff, and half-way through the scene the camera stopped again.

"Out of range," said the camera man carelessly, and lighted a cigarette. I had forgotten the circle of dots on the floor and crossed them.

I had eaten a large piece of the pie. There was a halt while another was brought, and the director, after an anxious look at the sun, used the interval in playing the scene through himself, falling through the trap-door, registering surprise and apprehension and panic at the proper points, and impressing upon me the way it was done. Then I tried it again.

All that afternoon I worked, black and blue from countless falls on the cement floor, perspiring in the intense heat, and eating no less than three large pies. They were cherry pies, and I had never cared much for them at any time.

When the light failed that evening the director, with a troubled frown, thoughtfully folded the working script and dismissed the camera man. Most of the actors in the other companies had gone; the wilderness of empty sets looked weird in the shadows. A boy appeared, caught the rats by their tails, and popped them back into their box.

"Well, that's all for to-day. We'll try it again to-morrow," the director said, not looking at me. "I guess you'll get the hang of it all right, after a while."

In my dressing-room I scrubbed the paint from my face and neck with vicious rubs. I knew I had failed miserably and my self-esteem smarted at the thought. Even if I had succeeded, I said bitterly, what was the fun in a life like that? No excitement, no applause, just hard work all day and long empty evenings with nothing to do.

Only two considerations prevented me from canceling my contract and quitting at once— I was getting two hundred dollars a week, and I would not admit to myself that I—I, who had been a success with William Gillette and a star with Carno—was a failure in the films Nevertheless, I was in a black mood that night, and when after dinner the waiter, bending deferentially at my elbow, insinuated politely, "The cherry pie is very good, sir," he fell back aghast at the language I used.

Work at the studio began at eight next morning, and I arrived very tired and ill-tempered because of waking so early. We began immediately on the same scene, and after I had ruined some more film by unexpectedly landing on a rat when I fell through the trap-door, we managed to get it done, to my relief. However, all that week, and the next, my troubles increased.

We played all the scenes which occurred in one set before we went on to the next set, so we were obliged to take the scenes at haphazard through the play, with no continuity or apparent connection. The interiors were all played on the stage, and most of the exteriors were taken "on location," that is, somewhere in the country. It was confusing, after being booted through a door, to be obliged to appear on the other side of it two days later, with the same expression, and complete the tumble begun fifteen miles away. It was still more confusing to play the scenes in reverse order, and I ruined three hundred feet of film by losing my hat at the end of a scene, when the succeeding one had already been played with my hat on.

At the end of the second week the comedy was all on the film and the director and I were being polite to each other with great effort. I was angry with every one and everything, my nerves worn thin with the early hours and unaccustomed work, and he was worried because I had made him a week late in producing the film. The day the negative was done Mack Sennett arrived from New York, and I met him with a jauntiness which was a hollow mockery of my real feeling.

"Well, they tell me the film's done," he said heartily, shaking my hand. "Now you're going to see yourself as others see you for the first time. Is the dark room ready? Let's go and see how you look on the screen."

The director led the way, and the three of us entered a tiny perfectly dark room. I could hear my heart beating while we waited, and talked nervously to cover the sound of it. Then there was a click, the shutter opened, and the picture sprang out on the screen. It was the negative, which is always shown before the real film is made, and on it black and white were reversed. It was several seconds before I realized that the black-faced man in white clothes, walking awkwardly before me, was myself. Then I stared in horror.

Funny? A blind man couldn't have laughed at it. I had ironed out entirely any trace of humor in the scenario. It was stiff, wooden, stupid. We sat there in silence, seeing the picture go on, seeing it become more awkward, more constrained, more absurd with every flicker. I felt as though the whole thing were a horrible nightmare of shame and embarrassment. The only bearable thing in the world was the darkness; I felt I could never come out into the light again, knowing I was the same man as the inane ridiculous creature on the film. Half-way through the picture Mr. Sennett took pity on me and stopped the operator.

"Well, Chaplin, you didn't seem to get it that time," he said. "What's wrong, do you suppose?"

"I don't know," I said.

"Yes, it's plain we can't release this," the director put in moodily. "Two thousand feet of film spoiled."

214

"Oh, damn your film!" I burst out in a fury, and rising with a spring which upset my chair I slammed open the door and stalked out. "Well, here is where I quit the pictures," I thought.

Mr. Sennett and the director overtook me before I reached my dressing-room and we talked it over. I felt that I would never make a moving-picture actor, but Mr. Sennett was more hopeful. "You're a crackerjack comedian," he said. "And you'll photograph well. All you need is to get camera-wise. We'll try you out in something else; I'll direct you, and you will get the hang of the work all right."

The director brought out a mass of scenarios which had been passed up to him by the scenario department and Mr. Sennett picked out one and ordered the working script of it made immediately. Next day we set to work together on it; Mr. Sennett patient, good-humored, considerate, coaching me over and over in every gesture and expression; I with a hard tense determination to make a success this time.

We worked another week on this second play, using every hour of good daylight. It was not entirely finished then, but enough was

215

done to give an idea of its success, and again the negative was sent to the dark room for review.

I went to see it with the sensations of dread and shrinking one feels at sight of a dentist's chair, and my worst fears were justified. The film was worse than the first one—utterly stupid and humorless.

CHAPTER XXVIII

In which I introduce an innovation in motion-picture
    production; appropriate an amusing mustache;
    and wager eighty dollars on three hours' work.

"WELL, what are we going to do about it?"
Mr. Sennett asked, when the flicker of the second film had ceased and we knew it a worse
failure than the first. "Looks hopeless,
doesn't it?"

"Yes," I said, with a sinking heart, for after
all I had had a flicker of hope for success this
time. We had both worked hard, and now we
were tired and discouraged. I went alone to
my dressing-room, shut the door and sat down
to think it over.

The trouble with the films, I decided, was
lack of spontaneity. I was stiff; I took all
the surprise out of the scenes by anticipating
the next motion. When I walked against a
tree, I showed that I knew I would hit it, long
before I did. I was so determined to be funny
that every muscle in my body was stiff and
serious with the strain. And then that con-

217

founded clicking of the camera and the effort it took to keep from looking at it—and the constant fear of spoiling a foot of film.

"So you're a failure," I said, looking at myself in the mirror. "You're a failure; no good; down and out. You can't make a cinema film. You're beaten by a click and an inch of celluloid. You *are* a rotter, no mistake!"

I was so furious at that that I smashed the mirror into bits with my fist. I walked up and down the dressing-room, hating myself and the camera and the film and the whole detestable business. I thought of haughtily stalking out and telling Mr. Sennett I was through with the whole thing; I was going back to London, where I was appreciated. Then I knew he would be glad to let me go; he would say to himself that I was no good in the pictures, and I would always know it was true. My vanity ached at the thought. No matter how much success I made, no matter how loud the audience applauded, I would always say to myself, "Very well for you, but you know you failed in the cinemas."

With a furious gesture I grabbed my hat and went out to find Mr. Sennett. He was on the stage watching the work of another company. I walked up to him in a sort of cold rage and said, "See here, Mr. Sennett, I can succeed in this beastly work. I know I can. You let me have a chance to do things the way I want to and I'll show you."

"I don't know what I can do. You've had the best scenarios we've got, and we haven't hurried you," he said reasonably. "You know the rest of the companies get out two reels a week, and we've taken three weeks to do what we've done with you—about a reel and a half."

"Yes, but the conditions are all wrong," I hurried on. "Rehearsing over and over, and no chance to vary an inch, and then that clicking beginning just when I start to play. And I miss a cane. I have to have a cane to be funny."

It must have sounded childish enough. Mr. Sennett looked at me in surprise.

"You can have a cane, if that's what you want. But I don't know how you are going to make pictures without rehearsing and without a camera," he said.

"I want to make up my own scenarios as I go along. I just want to go out on the stage and be funny," I said. "And I want the camera to keep going all the time, so I can forget about it."

"Oh, see here, Chaplin, you can't do that. Do you know what film costs? Four cents a foot, a thousand feet of film. You'd waste thousands of dollars' worth of it in a season. You see that yourself. Great Scott, man, you can't take pictures that way!"

"You give me a chance at it, and I'll show you whether I can or not," I replied. "Let me try it, just for a day or so, just one scene. If the film's spoiled, I'll pay for it myself."

We argued it out for a long time. The notion seemed utterly crazy to Mr. Sennett, but after all I had made a real success in comedy, and his disappointment must have been great at my failure on the films. Finally he consented to let me try making pictures my way, on condition that I should pay the salary of the operator and the cost of the spoiled film.

That night I walked up and down the street for hours, planning the outlines of a scenario and the make-up I would wear. My cane, of course, and the loose baggy trousers which are always funny on the stage, I don't know why.

I debated a long time about the shoes. My feet are small, and I thought perhaps they might seem funnier in tight shoes, under the baggy trousers. At last, however, I decided on the long, flat, floppy shoes, which would trip me up unexpectedly.

These details determined upon, I was returning to my hotel when suddenly I discovered I was hungry, and remembered that I had eaten no dinner. I dropped into a cafeteria for a cup of coffee, and there I saw a mustache. A little clipped mustache, worn by a very dignified solemn gentleman who was eating soup. He dipped his spoon into the bowl and the mustache quivered apprehensively. He raised the spoon and the mustache drew back in alarm. He put the soup to his lips and the mustache backed up against his nose and clung there.

It was the funniest thing I had ever seen. I choked my coffee, gasped, finally laughed outright. I must have a mustache like that!

Next day, dressed in the costume I had chosen, I glued the mustache to my lip before the dressing-room mirror, and shouted at the reflection. It was funny; it was uproariously funny! It waggled when I laughed, and I

221

laughed again. I went out on the stage still laughing, and followed by a shout of mirth from every one who saw me. I tripped on my cane, fell over my shoes, got the camera man to shouting with mirth. A crowd collected to watch me work, and I plunged into my first scene in high spirits.

I played the scene over and over, introducing funnier effects each time. I enjoyed it thoroughly, stopping every time I got out of the range of the camera to laugh again. The other actors, watching behind the camera, held their sides and howled, as my old audiences had done when I was with Carno. "This," I said to myself triumphantly. "This is going to be a success!"

When the camera finally stopped clicking all my old self-confidence and pride had come back to me. "Not so bad, what?" I said, triumphantly twirling my cane, and in sheer good spirits I pretended to fall against the camera, wringing a shout of terror from the operator. Then, modestly disclaiming the praises of the actors, though indeed I felt they were less than I deserved, I went whistling to my dressing-room.

"How soon do you want to see the film, Mr. Chaplin?" the operator asked, tapping at my door while I was changing into street clothes.

"Just as soon as you can have it, old top," I replied cheerfully. "Oh, by the way, how many feet did we use?"

"Little over two thousand," he called back, and I heard the sound of his retreating feet.

A little over two thousand! At four cents a foot! Eighty dollars! I felt as though a little cold breeze was blowing on my back. Nearly a month's salary with Carno wagered on the success of three hours' work! After all, I thought, I was not sure how the film would turn out; the beastly machine might not see the humor of my acting, good as it had been. I finished dressing in a hurry, and went out to find Mr. Sennett and show him the film in the dark room.

I sat on the edge of my chair in the dark room, waiting for the picture to flash on the screen, thinking of that eighty dollars, which alternately loomed large as a fortune and sank into insignificance. If the picture was good— But suppose it, too, was a failure! Then I would be stranded in California, thousands of

223

miles from home, and where would I get the eighty dollars?

The shutter clicked open and the negative began to flicker on the screen. I saw myself, black-faced, with a little white mustache and enormous white shoes, walking in great dignity across the patch of light. I saw myself trip over my shoes. I saw the mustache quiver with alarm. I saw myself stop, look wise, twirl my cane knowingly, and hit myself on the nose. Then, suddenly in the stillness, I heard a loud chuckle from Mr. Sennett. The picture was good. It was very good.

"Well, Chaplin, you've done it! By George, you've certainly got the comedy! It's a corker!" Mr. Sennett said, clapping me heartily on the back as we came out of the dark room. "You've wasted a lot of film, but hang the film! You're worth it! Go on and finish this up. I'd like to release it next week."

CHAPTER XXIX

In which I taste success in the movies; develop a new aim in life; and form an ambitious project.

"WE'LL use the third scene," Mr. Sennett said to the camera operator. "How long will it run?"

"About two hundred feet," the operator replied.

"Well, keep it and throw away the rest. Think you can finish two good reels this week?" Mr. Sennett asked, turning to me.

"Watch me!" I responded airily, and my heart gave a great jump. They were paying me two hundred dollars a week and were willing to throw away thousands of feet of film in addition to get my comedies. "There's a fortune in this business! A fortune!" I thought.

My ambition soared at that moment to dazzling heights. I saw myself retiring, after five or ten years in the business, with a fortune of ten thousand pounds—yes, even twenty thousand!

225

The comedy was finished that week; I worked every day, during every moment when the light was good, not stopping for luncheon or to rest. I enjoyed the work; the even click-click-click of the camera, running steadily, was a stimulant to me; my ideas came thick and fast. I sketched in my mind the outlines of a dozen comedies, to be played later. I remembered all the funny things I had seen or heard and built up rough scenarios around them. I woke in the night, chuckling at a new idea that occurred to me.

When my first comedy was released it was a great success. The producers demanded more, quickly. I was already working on *Caught in the Rain.* I followed it the next week with *Laughing Gas.* They all went big.

Every morning when I reached the stage in make-up the actors who were to play with me stood waiting to learn what their parts were to be. I myself did not always know, but when I had limbered up a bit by a jig or clog dance and the camera began to click, ideas came fast enough.

I told the other actors how to play their parts, played them myself to show how it

226

should be done; played my own part enthusiastically, teased the camera man, laughed and whistled and turned handsprings. The clicking camera took it all in; later, in the negative room, we chose and cut and threw away film, picking out the best scenes, rearranging the reels, shaping up the final picture to be shown on the screens. I liked it all; I was never still a minute in the studio and never tired.

The only time I was quiet was while I was making up. Then I thought sometimes of my early days in England, of Covent Garden, and my mother and my year with William Gillette. "Life's a funny thing," I said to myself. Then I made up as a baker, ordered a wagonload of bread-dough and flour and went out and romped through it hilarious, shouting with laughter whenever I was out of range of the camera. The result was *Dough and Dynamite,* and it clinched what I then thought was my success in the movies.

At first when my pictures began to appear in the moving-picture houses I took great delight in walking among the crowds in front of the doors, idly twirling my cane and listening to the comments on my comedies. I liked to go inside, too, and hear the audiences laugh at the comical figure I cut on the screen. That was the way I got my first real ambition in moving-picture work. I still have it. I want to make people chuckle.

Audiences laugh in two ways. Upon the stage, in all the tense effort of being funny behind the footlights, I had never noticed that. But one night, packed with the crowd in a small, dark moving-picture house, watching the flickering screen, listening for the response of the people around me, I suddenly realized it.

I had wedged into a crowded house to see my latest film. It was a rough-and-tumble farce; the audience had been holding its sides and shrieking hysterically for five minutes. "Oh, ho!" I was saying to myself. "You're getting 'em, old top, you're getting 'em!" Suddenly the laughter stopped.

I looked around dismayed. I could see a hundred faces, white in the dim light, intent on the picture—and not a smile on any of them. I looked anxiously at the screen. There was Charlie Chaplin in his make-up standing still. Standing still in a farce! I wondered how I had ever let a thing like that get past the negative. The house was still; I could hear the click of the unrolling film.

Then on the screen I saw myself turn slowly; saw my expression become grim and resolute; saw myself grip my cane firmly and stalk away. I was going after the husky laborer who had stolen my beer.

Then it came—a chuckle, a deep hearty "Ha! Ha! Ha!" It spread over the crowd like a wave; the house rocked with it.

"That's it! That's what I want, that's what I want!" I said. I got out quickly to think it over. I had to crowd past the knees of a dozen people to do it, and not one of them glared at me. They were still chuckling.

I walked back to my hotel with my cane tucked under my arm and my hands in my pockets. That was the thing—the chuckle! Any kind of laughter is good; any kind of laughter will get the big salaries. But a good, deep, hearty chuckle is the thing that warms a man's heart; it's the thing that makes him your friend; it's the thing that shows, when you get it, that you have a real hold on your audience. I have worked for it ever since.

After that I visited the picture houses night

after night, watching for that chuckle, planning ways to get it. I was never recognized by strangers, and more than once some one asked me what I thought of Charlie Chaplin. I do not recall that I ever told the truth. In fact, I was not thinking much about Charlie Chaplin in those days; I was thinking of his work and his success and his growing bank-account.

I had come into the business at the height of its first big success. Fortunes were being made overnight in it; producers could not turn out film fast enough to satisfy the clamoring public. The studios were like gambling houses in the wild fever of play. Money was nothing; it was thrown away by hundreds, by thousands. "Give us the film, give us the film! To hell with the expense!" was the cry. I heard of small tailors, of street-car motormen, who had got into the game with a few hundred dollars and now were millionaires. In six months I was smiling at my early notion of making fifty thousand dollars.

Sidney, who was still in vaudeville, came to Los Angeles about that time, and I met him at the train with one of the company's big automobiles. The same old reliable Sidney with

230

his sound business sense. He had figured out the trend of affairs and was already negotiating with the Essanay company for a good contract with them, going deliberately into the work I had blundered into by accident.

"There's a fortune in this if it's handled right, Charlie," he said.

"A fortune? If this holds out, if I can keep up my popularity, I'll have a cool half million before I quit, my lad! Keep your eye piped for your Uncle Charlie!" I said gaily.

CHAPTER XXX

In which I see myself as others see me; learn many surprising things about myself from divers sources; and see a bright future ahead.

Sid laughed.

"Well, have it your way, old top!" he said. "What will you do when you get your half million?"

"Do? I'll quit. I'll be satisfied," I said. "You can't keep 'em coming forever, and I don't expect it. I'll give them the best I have as long as I can, and then—curtains! But I wager we keep out of the Actor's Home, what?"

Sid laughed again. "There's money in the movies, Charlie," he said. "Half a million? You wait a year. Your popularity hasn't begun."

He was right. In a world where so many people are troubled and unhappy, where women lead such dreary lives as my mother did when I was a boy, where men spend their days in hard unwilling toil and children starve as I starved in the London slums, laughter is

232

precious. People want to laugh; they long to forget themselves for half an hour in the hearty joy of it. Every night on a hundred thousand motion-picture screens my floppy shoes and tricky cane and eloquent mustache were making people laugh, and they remembered them and came to laugh again. Suddenly, almost overnight, Charlie Chaplin became a fad, a craze.

My first idea of it came one night when I was returning from a hard day's work at the studio. It had been a hot day; I had worked thirteen hours in a mask of grease paint under the blazing heat of the Southern California sun intensified by a dozen huge reflectors before the inexorable click-click-click of the camera, driven by the necessity of finishing the reel while the light lasted. My exuberance of spirit had waned by noon; by four o'clock I was driving myself by sheer will-power, doggedly, determinedly being funny. At seven we finished the reel. At nine we had got the film in shape in the negative room, and I had nothing to do till next morning but get my ideas together for a new comedy.

I was slumped in a heap in the tonneau of the director's car hurrying to my hotel and thinking that the American system of built-in baths had its advantages, when we ran up to a crowd that almost stopped street traffic. The sidewalk was jammed for half a block; men were standing up in automobiles to get a better view of whatever was happening. My chauffeur stopped.

"What's the row?" I asked one of the men in the crowd.

"Charlie Chaplin's in there!" he said excitedly, jumping on the running-board and craning his neck to look over the heads of the men in front of him.

"Really?" I said. I stood up and looked. There in front of a moving-picture theater was Charlie Chaplin, sure enough—shoes, baggy trousers, mustache and all. The chap was walking up and down as well as he could in the jam of people, twirling his cane and tripping over his shoes. Policemen were trying to clear the sidewalk, but the crowd was mad for a glimpse of him. I stood there looking at him with indescribable emotions.

"That's funny," I said after a minute. The

234

man on the running-board had only half heard me.

"Funny? I should say he is! He's the funniest man in America!" he said. "They say he gets a hundred dollars a day and only works when he's stewed."

"Well, well! Really!" I said.

"I guess that's right, too," he went on. "He acts like it on the screen, don't he? Say, have you seen his latest picture? Man, it's a knockout! When he fell into that sewer—! They faked the sewer, of course, but say—! I like to of fell out of my seat!"

We had not faked the sewer. It was a thoroughly real sewer. But I drove on to my hotel without explaining. The whole situation was too complex.

Within a week half the motion-picture houses in Los Angeles had the only original and genuine Charlie Chaplin parading up and down before them. I grew so accustomed to meeting myself on the street that I started in surprise every time I looked into a mirror without my make-up. Overnight, too, a thousand little figures of Charlie Chaplin in plaster sprang up and crowded the shop windows. I could not buy a tooth-brush without reaching over a counter packed with myself to do it.

It was odd, walking up and down the streets, eating in cafés, hearing Charlie Chaplin talked about, seeing Charlie Chaplin on every hand and never being recognized as Charlie Chaplin. I had a feeling that all the world was cross-eyed, or that I was a disembodied spirit. But that did not last long. A plague of reporters descended on the studios soon, like whatever it was that fell upon Egypt. Then the world seemed more topsy-turvy than ever, for here I was, an actor, dodging reporters!

Not that I have any dislike of reporters. Indeed, in the old days I asked nothing better than to get one to listen to me and often planned for days to capture one's attention. But that's another of life's little jokes. A man who tries hard enough for anything will always get it—after he has stopped wanting it.

I had to turn out the film, hundreds of feet of it every week, and it must be made while the light lasted. The gambling fever had spent itself in the picture business; directors were beginning to count costs. To stop my company half an hour meant a waste of several hundred

236

dollars. And every morning half a dozen reporters waited for me to give them "Just a few minutes, Mr. Chaplin!"

I took to dodging in and out of the studio like a hunted man. Did I stop to give a harried and unwary opinion upon something I knew nothing whatever about, next Sunday I beheld with staring eyes a full-page story on my early life, told in the first person. At last, in the pressure of getting out two new comedies in a hurry, I escaped interviews for nearly three weeks. We were working overtime; it was late in the fall, when the weather was uncertain and the light bad. We would start at five in the morning to get to our "location" in the country by sunrise, only to have the morning foggy. Then we hurried back to the studio to work under artificial light, and the afternoon was sunny. It was a hard nerve-racking three weeks and our tempers were not improved when, at the end of the last day, we tried out the negative as usual and found the camera had leaked light and ruined nearly a reel of film.

Hurrying off the stage to get a quick supper, so that I could return and make up as much lost time as possible that night, I encountered on the studio steps a thin young man in a derby, who did not recognize me.

"Say, is it true Chaplin's crazy?" he asked.

"Crazy?" I said.

"Yes. He hasn't released a film for over a month and I can't get hold of him here. They say he's raving crazy, confined in an asylum."

"He is not," I said. Then the humor of the thing struck me. "He isn't violent yet," I said, "but he may be, any minute."

Half an hour later two morning papers telephoned the director for confirmation of the report, which he denied emphatically and profanely. No story appeared in the papers, but I have since been solemnly told by a hundred people who "have it straight" that Chaplin is, or has been, confined in the California Hospital for the Insane.

Behind all this flurry of comment and conjecture I was working, working hard, turning out the best film I could devise, with my mind always on the problem of getting that deep, hearty chuckle from the audience. I did not always get it, but I did get laughs. And my contract with the Keystone company was running out; I saw still brighter prospects ahead.

238

CHAPTER XXXI

In which the moving-picture work palls on me; I
make other plans, am persuaded to abandon them
and am brought to the brink of a deal in high
finance.

THE reorganization among the producers of
motion pictures, which followed the era of
mushroom companies sprung up ´overnight,
making fabulous fortunes, wildly, in the first
scramble for quick profits and going down
again in the general chaos, was still under way
when my contract with the Keystone company,
expired.

Millions of laughs, resounding every night
in hundreds of moving-picture theaters had set
producers to bidding for me. I received offers
of incredible sums from some companies; lavish
promises of stock from others. The situation,
I felt, required the mind of a financier. I
called in Sidney.

After a great deal of consideration, we decided to accept the offer of the Essanay com-

pany, as combining in due proportion size of salary and security of its payment. My contract called for a thousand dollars a day, also a percentage on my films.

A thousand dollars a day! Two hundred pounds every twenty-four hours! At the moment of signing the contract a feeling of unreality came over me. It seemed incredible. Only five years ago I had been cockily congratulating myself on wringing ten pounds a week from Carno!

I returned to Los Angeles in the highest spirits and set to work again. A small company, three actors and a score of "supers," was got together for me. The stage, a rough board structure large enough for a dozen "sets," built near the bridge of the street railway between Los Angeles and Pasadena, was turned over to me and my company. Here, on a little side street of tumble-down sheds half buried in tangles of dusty woods, I shut myself in behind the high wooden wall of the studio through the long hot summer and worked at being funny.

Every morning, as soon as the light was right for the pictures, I arrived at the studio

and got into my make-up, racking my brain
the while for a funny idea. The company stood
waiting in the white-hot glare of the big canvas
reflectors; the camera was ready; at the other
end of the long-distance wire the company
clamored for film, more film and still more. I
must go out on the stage and be funny, be
funny as long as the light lasted.

"The whole thing's in your hands, Chaplin,"
the managers said cheerfully. "Give us the
film, that's all we ask."

I gave them the film. All day long,
tumbling down-stairs, falling into lakes, collid-
ing with moving vans, upsetting stepladders,
sitting in pails of wall-paper paste, I heard it
click-click-clicking past the camera shutter.
At night, in the negative room, I checked and
cut and revised it. And all the time I searched
my mind for funny ideas.

Now, nothing in the world is more rare than
an idea, except a funny idea. The necessity of
working out a new one every day, the responsi-
bility of it and the labor so wore upon me that
by fall I had come to a stern determination. I
would leave the moving pictures. I would
leave them as soon as I had a million dollars.

"If this keeps up another year I will be a millionaire," I said to myself one evening, lying on the cement floor of the basement set, where I had gone in my search for a cool spot to rest. "Then I'll quit. I will quit and write a book. I never have written a book, and I might as well. But not a funny book. Ye gods, no!"

After all, I had had my share of the limelight, as I had always known, even in my worst days, that I would some day. I had made my success on the legitimate stage with William Gillette. I had made my success and my money in the moving pictures in America. I was still in my twenties. Why not leave the stage altogether, settle down on some snug little ranch and write? It might be jolly fun to be an author. By jove, I'd do it!

My arrangement with the Essanay people had been for only a year—Sidney's prudent idea. The contract was expiring in a few months; already I was receiving offers from other companies. I would refuse them all; yes, I would quit with less than a million dollars. Three-quarters of a million would be plenty. Lying there on the cool cement floor, still in my baggy trousers, with the grease paint on my face, I stretched my legs and waggled my floppy shoes contentedly. Jove, the relief of never being funny again!

"Charlie, old boy, don't be a gory idiot!" Sid protested, when I told him my project. "Why, you can make a fortune at this. Hutchinson, of the Mutual, is in town right now; I was talking to him last night. They'll make you an offer—you can get fifty offers that will beat anything you've dreamed about. You can be the highest-paid movie actor in the world."

"What's a million more or less, old man?" I said airily, though I began to waver. "I've made my pile. I want to write a book."

"How do you know you can write a book?" Sidney returned. "Of all the bally rot! D'you want to go off somewhere and never be heard of again? Or have you got another notion that William Gillette's going to take you to America?"

It was the first time Sidney had ever mentioned that affair since the day he had bought me clothes and so got me out of the London hospital and taken me home. I had told him all about it then.

CHARLIE CHAPLIN'S OWN STORY

It struck me he was probably right. It has
been my experience that he usually is.

"All right," I said. "Your contract's up
with the Essanay, too. Come over and manage
things for me and I'll stay with the moving
pictures."

He agreed and we began to consider which
company I should choose. The moving-picture
business is standardized now; a few big companies practically divide the field between
them. The various departments of the work
have been segregated also, a producing company turning its films over to a releasing
company which markets them. What we most
desired was to make a connection with a big
releasing company, since if I got a percentage
of the profits which we meant to stand out for,
the marketing of the films was most important.

I felt greatly relieved when my contract
expired and I drove away from the studio for
the last time, free for some weeks from the
obligation of being funny. Sidney was busily
negotiating with several companies, consider-
ing their offers and their advantages from our
view-point. I was idle and care-free; I might
do what I liked. I whistled cheerfully to my-

self, swinging my cane as I walked down to
dinner that night, facing the prospect before
me with happy anticipation.

In a week I discovered that the one thing I
most wanted to do was to be acting. A thousand bright ideas for comedy situations rushed
into my mind; I longed to put on my make-up
again, to smell the piny odor of the studio in
the hot sun, to hear the click of the camera. I
looked regretfully at the old signs on the movie
theaters; no new Chaplin pictures were being
released. I was eager to be back at work.

Each night I discussed more eagerly with
Sidney the different companies we were con-
sidering. At last, after a great many talks
with Mr. Hutchinson, we privately decided on
the Mutual as offering the best advantages.
This decision, however, we prudently refrained
from mentioning until after Mr. Caulfield, the
personal representative of the Mutual's president, Mr. Freuler, should come to Los Angeles
and make us a definite money offer.

Mr. Caulfield promptly arrived, and Sidney
undertook the negotiations with him, keeping
me in reserve to bring up at the proper time.
I relied a great deal upon Sidney; I knew

myself entirely capable in handling theatrical managers, but I had greater confidence in Sidney's handling of business men. I awaited somewhat nervously my share in the arrangements.

One night my cue came. Sidney telephoned up from down-stairs. "I'm bringing Caulfield up," he said. "He offers ten thousand a week and royalties. I'm holding out for two hundred and fifty thousand dollars bonus on signing the contract. Stick at that if you can, but whatever you do, don't take less than one hundred and twenty-five thousand dollars."

CHAPTER XXXII

In which I see success in my grasp; proudly consider the heights to which I have climbed; and receive an unexpected shock.

SIDNEY came in a moment later, bringing Mr. Caulfield. Like Mr. Hutchinson, like, indeed, most of the men handling the affairs of the big motion-picture corporations, Mr. Caulfield is a keen, quick-witted business man. Producing and selling moving-picture films is now a business as matter of fact as dealing in stocks and bonds; there is nothing of the theatrical manager about the men who control it.

"Well, Mr. Chaplin, your brother and I have been reaching an agreement about your contract with us," he said briskly. "We will give you a salary of ten thousand dollars a week and royalties that should double that figure." He mentioned the per cent. agreed upon, as I assented.

"More than that, we are planning to create a separate producing company, subsidiary to

247

the Mutual, which will be its releasing company, and to call the new concern the Lone Star company—you to be the lone star. The new company will build its own studios at Santa Barbara, and it will give you the finest supporting cast that money can hire." He mentioned a few of the actors he had in mind, and I agreed heartily to his suggestions. They were good actors; I knew I could do good work with them.

"That is the offer as it stands," he concluded. "Half a million dollars in salary, another half-million, probably, in royalties. That depends on the amount of film the Lone Star company turns out. We'll give you every facility for producing it; the Mutual will handle the releases. We will be ready to start work as soon as you sign the contract."

"Then," I said pleasantly, "we need only decide the amount of the bonus to be paid me for signing it."

"Frankly, Mr. Chaplin, I am not authorized to offer you a bonus," he replied. "We don't do that. And we feel that in organizing your own company, building studios, giving you such a supporting cast, we are doing all that

248

is possible, in addition to the record-breaking salary and royalties we are willing to pay you."

"On the other hand, you must consider that I have other offers," I answered. "Frankly, also, I imagine the size of the bonus paid me will decide which company I choose. I want two hundred and fifty thousand. We both know I am worth it to any company."

It was a deadlock. The old thrill of my dealing with Carno came back to me while we talked. In the end he left, the matter still undecided.

There were many interviews after that. I still believe that it might have been possible, by holding out longer, to get that amount, but I was eager to begin work again, and besides, as Mr. Caulfield pointed out, the sooner we began releasing films the sooner the royalties would begin coming in.

In the end we compromised on a cash bonus of one hundred and fifty thousand dollars, and an agreement on my part to secure the company for that payment by allowing them to insure my life for half a million dollars. We made application for the insurance policy and I was examined by the insurance company's physician, so that there might be no delay in closing the arrangements with the Mutual and beginning work.

"Fit as a fiddle, sir; fit as a fiddle!" the doctor said, thumping my chest. He felt the muscles of my arms approvingly. "Outdoor life, outdoor life and exercise, they're the best medicine in the world. What is your occupation, sir, if I may ask?"

"I'm a sort of rough-and-tumble acrobat," I said. "A moving-picture actor."

"Well, bless my soul! Chaplin, of course! I didn't get the name. Yes, yes, I see the resemblance now. I'm glad to meet you, sir. That last comedy of yours—when you fell into the lake—" He chuckled.

In great good spirits, then, we set out for New York, where the contract was to be signed by Mr. Freuler and myself and the final details settled.

Ten years ago I had been a starving actor on the Strand, a percocious youngster with big dreams and an empty stomach. Now I was on my way to New York and a salary of five hundred and twenty thousand dollars a year. Then I had been hungry for the slightest recognition;

250

CHARLIE CHAPLIN'S OWN STORY

I had schemed and posed and acted a part with
every one I met, craving a glance of admira-
tion or envy to encourage my really tremulous
hopes of one day succeeding; I had deceived
myself with flattery to keep up my spirits.
Now my name was known wherever moving
pictures were shown throughout the world; a
million hearty laughs applauded me every day.

I felt that I had arrived and I was happy.

From New York I hastened to cable my
mother the dazzling news—my poor, pretty
little mother, older now and never really strong
since the terrible days when we starved together
in a London garret. She can not come to
America because she can not stand the sea trip,
but from the first I had written her at great
length about my tremendous success, and when
my comedies appeared in England she went for
the first time to the cinema houses, and wrote
that it was good to see me again and my comedy
work was splendid; she was proud of me.

We were to sign the contract in the offices of
the Mutual company in New York. When we
stepped into that suite of richly furnished
rooms, to be ushered at once into the presence
of the president of this multi-million-dollar

251

parent corporation, I had one fleeting thought of myself, ten years before, wearily tramping the Strand from agent's office to agent's office, the scorn of the grimiest cockney office boy.

The curious twists and turns of chance in those old days should have prepared me for the shock I received when I met Mr. Freuler, but they had not done so. I felt so secure, so satisfied with myself and the world as I stepped into his private office.

"I'm sorry, Mr. Chaplin," he said when Mr. Caulfield had introduced us and we were seated. "I'm afraid there will be a hitch in the paying of that bonus. The insurance company has refused to issue your policy."

CHAPTER XXXIII

In which I realize my wildest dreams of fortune; ponder on the comedy tricks of life and conclude without reaching any conclusion.

"REFUSED to issue—impossible!" I cried, starting in my chair. With the swiftness of a knife stab I saw myself stopped at the very moment of my greatest success, fighting, struggling, hoping—and dying swiftly of some inexorable, concealed disease. Why, I had never felt better in my life!

"Yes, we received their refusal only this morning. On account of your extra-hazardous occupation they will not carry a policy for such a large sum," said Mr. Freuler. "I'm sorry, but I'm afraid it will hold matters up until we have found a company which will insure you or distributed the amount among a number of companies."

I laughed. I felt that Fate had shot her last bolt at me and missed. Extra-hazardous, of course! I had grown accustomed to the staff of nurses waiting at every large studio during thrilling scenes. I had trained myself by long practise to come comically through every dangerous mishap with as little danger of broken bones as possible. That was part of the work of being funny.

"Oh, very well," I said. "What shall we do to arrange the matter?"

It was a question which occupied our thoughts for several days. No large company would insure my life against the hazards of my comedies. We did, however, finally hit upon a way of solving the problem, and at last, worth nearly half a million dollars to the Mutual company if I died and much more if I lived, I signed the contract and received my check for one hundred and fifty thousand dollars.

I did it, as was fitting, to the sound of a clicking camera, for the Mutual company, with great enterprise, filmed the event, that audiences the world over might see me in my proper person, wielding the fateful pen. It was a moment during which I should have felt a degree of emotion, that moment at which the pen point, scrawling "Charles Chaplin," made me worth another million dollars. But the click-click-click of the camera as the operator turned the crank made the whole thing unreal to me. I was careful only to register the proper expression.

"Well—it's finished. What about your half-million now?" Sidney said affectionately when, my copy of the contract safely tucked into my breast pocket, we set off down the street together. "You'll quit, will you, with half a million! You'll never leave the moving pictures, my lad!"

"Have it your own way, old scamp," I said. "You would, anyway. Just the same I would like to write a book. I wager I could do it, with half a chance. By the way, there's another thing I'd like to do—"

Then I had all the pleasure and delight of feeling rich, of which the camera had robbed me while I signed my contract. At last I had an opportunity to repay Sidney the money part of the debt I have owed him since he came to my rescue so many times when we were boys. He could not refuse half of the bonus money, which he had worked so hard to get for me, and that check for seventy-five thousand dollars gave me more pleasure than I can recall receiving from any other money I have ever handled.

255

So I came back to the Pacific coast to begin my work with the Mutual company. I am now an assured success in moving-picture comedy work and I am most proud of it. There is great cause for pride in keeping thousands of persons laughing. There is the satisfaction, also, of having attained, through lucky chance and accident, the goal on which I set my eyes so many years ago.

But I have no golden rule for such attainment to offer any one. I have worked—yes, to the limit of my ability—but so have many other men who have won far less reward than I. Whether you call it chance, fate or providence, to my mind the ruling of men's lives is in other hands than theirs.

If Sidney had not returned to London I might have become a thief in the London streets. If William Gillette had brought me to America I might have become a great tragic actor. If the explosion in the glass factory had been more violent I might have been buried in a pauper's grave. Now, by a twist of public fancy, which sees great humor in my best work, and less in the best work of other men who are toiling as hard as I, I have become Charlie

Chaplin, "the funniest man in America," and a millionaire.

What rules our destinies in this big comedy, the world? I do not know. I know only that it is good, whatever happens, to laugh at it.

Meantime, I am working on a new comedy. I am always working on a new comedy. I have a whole stage to myself, a stage of bare new boards that smell of turpentine in the hot sunshine, covered with dozens of sets—drawing-rooms, bedrooms, staircases, basements, roofs, fire-escapes, laundries, baker-shops, barrooms—everything.

As soon as the light is strong enough I arrive in my big automobile, falling over the steps when I get out to amuse the chauffeur. I coat my face with light brown paint, paste on my mustache, get into my floppy shoes, loop my trousers up about my waist, clog-dance a bit. Then the camera begins to click and I begin to be funny. I enjoy my comedies; they seem the funniest things on earth while I am playing them. I laugh, the other actors laugh, the director fans himself with his straw hat and laughs; the camera man chuckles aloud.

Dozens of ideas pop into my mind as I play;

I play my parts each with a fresh enthusiasm, changing them, inventing, devising, accidentally producing unexpected effects, carefully working out others, enjoying every moment of it.

When the light falls in the evening I may sit a while, for coolness, in the basement set, where the glare of the reflectors has not beat all 'day. Then sometimes I think of the tricks fate has played with me since the days I clog-danced for Mr. Hawkins, and I wonder why and what the meaning of it all may be. But I never decide.

THE END